contents

Acknowledgements

■ We are very grateful to Dean's employers BakeMark International, the sales organisation representing parent company CSM's bakery supplies business, for all their support and assistance. In the course of his job, Dean visits a wide range of bakeries and pâtisseries around the world. Many of the bakers he has met along the way have inspired the recipes developed for this book.

Another talented baker, Marcus Braun of the New Zealand Baking Training Centre at the Christchurch Polytechnic Institute of Technology (CPIT), assisted in the testing of every recipe for this book and also flew to Auckland to help style the baked goods for the photography. CPIT allowed Dean and Marcus to test-bake the recipes on campus, and for that we thank them.

Our photographer, Aaron McLean, was a delight to work with, and we hope he goes on to shoot many more books. The photography is a major undertaking, and Moffat NZ's test bakery in Mt Wellington, Auckland, was generously loaned to us for the photo shoots. We are very grateful for their support and good cheer when we completely took over their showroom.

William Chen, *Cuisine* magazine's brilliant art director, helped with the styling and propping and his inimitable good taste shines through, ensuring our food looks superb. Babushka Antiques, Cavit & Co, Corso de Fiore, Cranfields, Destination Home, Galtons of Parnell, La Cigale and The Homestore all provided wonderful props. Treasures from the private collections of the Lewis/Walsh family, Patricia Stevens and Alexa Johnston were graciously lent. Thank you all.

Bob Ross of Tandem Press initially had the wisdom to accept our idea for another baking book, and we have been thrilled subsequently to work with the talented team at Random House: publisher Tom Beran, editor Claire Gummer and designer Trevor Newman.

Also many thanks to all Dean's friends and baking colleagues around the world for their ideas and constant support, and their willingness to embrace his baking philosophy: "Commitment, dedication, passion – and a little fun."

Last but by no means least (although they sometimes don't think we notice), we thank our families for their loving support, patience and loyalty.

Dean Brettschneider and Lauraine Jacobs

taste
baking with flavour

Dean Brettschneider   Lauraine Jacobs

photography Aaron McLean

RANDOM HOUSE
NEW ZEALAND

To Vivien,

Thanks for baking such a storm. Keep it up !! All the best.

taste
baking with flavour

National Library of New Zealand
Cataloguing-in-Publication Data

Brettschneider, Dean.
Taste : baking with flavour / Dean Brettschneider,
Lauraine Jacobs.
Includes index.
ISBN 1-86941-684-8
1. Bread. 2. Cake. 3. Pastry. 4. Cookery.
I. Jacobs, Lauraine. II. Title.
641.815—dc 22

A RANDOM HOUSE BOOK
published by
Random House New Zealand
18 Poland Road, Glenfield, Auckland, New Zealand
www.randomhouse.co.nz

First published 2005

© 2005 text: Dean Brettschneider and Lauraine Jacobs;
photography: Aaron McLean
The moral rights of the authors have been asserted

ISBN 1 86941 684 8

Cover and text design: Trevor Newman
Printed in China

Foreword

■ From very simple origins, bakery foods have developed over the centuries to provide us with a rich variety of breads, cakes and pastries. Every region in every country has developed its own tastes, shapes and traditions. For those of us involved in the world of baking, this makes every day an adventure of taste, with the discovery of new ideas and new flavour combinations.

When I first met Dean Brettschneider, I was immediately struck by his infectious enthusiasm for all things baked. For Dean, it is not enough to have an ordinary bread roll with a meal — that roll must enhance the diner's eating experience; it must be part of the meal, not just an add-on. Dean possesses a missionary zeal to let all food-lovers know the wealth of wonderful breads that are available in the world. As we would choose a wine to go with a meal, surely we should also choose our bread to complement and enhance that meal?

More recently, I have had the opportunity to work with Dean as a colleague in BakeMark International, which works with many different types of food businesses across the world and helps them to develop their bakery and pâtisserie ranges. Dean has not only brought his vast enthusiasm and knowledge to our business; he has also helped make our day-to-day activities a real adventure in flavours and ideas. What's more, he has helped us move beyond the bakery to instil a love of baking in such places as restaurants, hotels and even fast-food and snack chains.

Baked food is universal and versatile. It can be eaten at any time of day, and it encompasses indulgent treats that are the height of luxury as well as highly nutritious staple foods. Baking has developed — from the essential bread recipe of flour, yeast and water and the fundamental cake recipe of flour, fat and sugar — to offer a huge range of flavours, textures, colours, shapes and aromas. In reading this book, you will enjoy a flavoursome adventure in baking in the great company of Dean Brettschneider and Lauraine Jacobs.

Andrew Adam, Marketing Manager

INTERNATIONAL
www.bakemarkinternational.com

Introduction

■ Fifty years ago, scientists thought that pills and capsules could become the food of the future. A small selection of these delicacies could be taken each day, providing all the nutrients that people needed.

But true food-lovers knew that this was never going to happen. Texture, colour, shapes, aroma and most importantly flavour were so highly prized that some kind of clinical prescription was never going to cut it. We all need to chew!

We are lucky that living in the 21st century has meant that a great many flavours and food experiences are available to us. Rapid increases in world travel, cross-cultural communication and development in technology mean we can experience an extraordinary range of exciting foods.

The world of baking reflects these diverse advances, and baking is enjoying a resurgence around the globe. More and more people are appreciating that there is nothing that can quite compare with the aromas that waft through the house, café or bakery when a baker is at work. The tantalising smells of freshly baked pies, breads, cakes or cookies stir up hunger and a longing to indulge in such treats.

There is much more to baking than merely sampling the results, rewarding as that is. The alchemy involved in creating delicious, appetising food has intrigued and inspired people everywhere — and none more so than the baker. Baking is an astonishing rich, diverse process. It is an art and also an exact science, combining creativity and precision. It is ancient and modern, drawing on both tradition and technology. If you are willing to work with your hands, baking is undeniably an intensely physical experience. An increasing number of bakers world-wide are returning to the artisanal craft of baking rather than the mechanised processes that have been developed in the age of speed and ease.

Taste – Baking with Flavour offers all that an experienced baker could possibly wish for to extend their horizons, and takes a new baker through the steps needed to enter the world of baking. This book contains recipes that have been inspired by world travels. It enables you to blend time-honoured techniques with innovative, appealing flavours so you can achieve great results in your own home or bakery. The wide range of interesting new recipes includes a few gluten-free and dairy-free goods, and every recipe guarantees great results. The cakes, pastries and breads are so delicious they will disappear in no time, but you can bake them again and again.

Anyway, practice makes perfect! Enjoy baking with flavour.

How It Works

■ Recipes have been divided into three chapters: Pastries, Pies and Tarts; Breads; and Cakes and Cookies. Each of these begins with essential techniques, basic recipes and 'How It Works' sections to boost the baker's knowledge and understanding. The more advanced recipes that follow will seem simple if you read through them before starting to bake (especially if you take a second read-through, noting anything you need to buy or prepare in advance). Each one features 'Keys to Success', and the accompanying photographs not only look good, they also provide a visual guide to the finished product. Supplementary sections complete the book with useful information on baking equipment, ingredients, formulas, measurements and vocabulary.

pastries, pies and tarts

Butter Puff Pastry (also called Flaky Pastry)

Butter Puff Pastry involves a longer process than its cousins Sweet, Short and Choux Pastry. It seems to take forever to build up the thin layers of dough and butter, and even the professionals sometimes buy ready-made puff pastry. However, the homemade kind is best. The more folds you make in the pastry, the more puff it produces during the baking.

300g bread flour
50g chilled butter
salt
150ml ice-cold water
1 teaspoon fresh lemon juice
225g chilled butter, for layering

■ Place the flour, 50g butter and salt in a large mixing bowl. Using your fingers, roughly break the butter into the flour. Add the water and lemon juice and then, using your hands, mix the ingredients to form a firm dough.

Tip the dough out onto a lightly floured bench and knead for 2–3 minutes. Form into a ball, cover with plastic wrap and allow to rest for 5–10 minutes. On a lightly floured bench, roll the dough out to a 25cm x 25cm square, approximately 1cm thick.

Ensure the 225g layering butter is the same soft, pliable consistency as the dough: this can be achieved by hitting the butter with a rolling pin until it is 17cm x 17cm. Then place it on the rolled-out dough.

Fold each corner of the dough into the centre to encase the layering butter (like an envelope), obtaining two layers of dough and one of butter.

Give the pastry four 'single turns' as described below.

Roll the pastry out to a rectangle 1cm thick. Imagine dividing the rectangle into thirds:

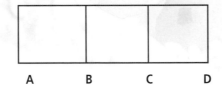

A   B   C   D

Fold line A to C, then fold line D to B to complete three layers of pastry.

Rest the pastry for 15–20 minutes in the refrigerator, covered with plastic wrap to prevent it from forming a dry skin.

Repeat three times, resting the pastry as described after each turn.

At this point you can either roll the pastry out to the required final thickness and refrigerate it for up to three days, or freeze it until you need it.

■ Makes enough pastry for 1 x 20cm round tart, including top and bottom

Roll and fold to achieve a 'single turn'.

Baking and Cooling

PRODUCT	TEMPERATURE	TIME
Unfilled puff pastry	220–230°C	18–20 minutes
Filled puff pastry (sweet)	215–220°C	20–25 minutes
Filled puff pastry (savoury)	220–225°C	25–30 minutes
Baked puff pastry (to reheat)	190–200°C	15–25 minutes

Times and temperatures will vary from oven to oven.

■ Once the Puff Pastry is out of the oven it should be cooled on a rack to avoid sweating. Pies should be allowed to cool slightly before being removed from their tins to prevent the pie shell from collapsing.

How It Works

■ Once the layers of dough are placed in a correctly preheated oven, the fat melts and the moisture within the dough begins to produce steam. The protein (gluten) in the dough begins to expand and separate, and the steam pushes the dough layers upwards. Once the Puff Pastry has reached its maximum volume and all the moisture within the dough has escaped, the protein begins to coagulate (set), giving the pastry its structure. If the pastry is taken out of the oven before coagulation (setting) is complete, the structure will collapse.

Keys to Success

■ Keep all your ingredients cool.

■ Use iced water in summer (do not put ice cubes in the dough; they will not dissolve during mixing).

■ When rolling the dough out for each fold, ensure that the open ends are folded back into the dough.

■ When rolling and folding your puff pastry, use as little dusting flour as possible. Brush away any excess flour before completing each fold.

■ It is advisable to thaw frozen pastry in the refrigerator overnight. Before rolling it out to its required thickness, let it stand at room temperature for approximately 30 minutes.

■ Store your puff pastry in plastic wrap to prevent it from drying out.

■ Adhere to the resting times stated to avoid shrinkage during baking.

■ Always rest puff pastry before baking, the longer the better (anywhere from 2–12 hours in the refrigerator). If you are resting it in the refrigerator, allow it to warm up before you put it in the oven.

Short and Sweet Pastry

The high proportion of butter in Short Pastry and its sister Sweet Pastry produces a soft, melt-in-the-mouth quality.

Short Pastry (also called Brisé Pastry)

240g standard flour
180g butter, at room temperature
salt
70ml ice-cold water

■ Place the flour, butter and salt in a large mixing bowl. Using your fingers, gently rub the ingredients together until they resemble rough breadcrumbs. Do not over-mix, or the heat from your fingers will begin to melt the butter. Add the water and mix until a dough is formed.

Wrap the pastry in plastic and refrigerate for 30 minutes or overnight. Gently re-work it before use, taking care to keep it cold and firm.

On a lightly floured bench, roll the pastry out to about 3mm thick or as required for your recipe.

Store the unbaked pastry in the refrigerator or freezer, unfilled or filled. It is advisable to thaw it in the refrigerator overnight. Before rolling it out to its required thickness, let it stand at room temperature for approximately 30 minutes.

■ Makes enough pastry for 7 x muffin-sized pies (as in French Apple Compote Pies)

Lining a Sweet Pastry flan tin.

Sweet Pastry (also called Sweet Shortcrust Pastry)

170g butter, softened
85g sugar
1 small egg
4 drops pure vanilla essence
zest of ½ lemon
260g standard flour

■ Gently beat the butter and sugar with a wooden spoon until it is light and creamy. Add the egg, vanilla and lemon, and mix until combined. Lastly, add the flour and mix to a paste. Stop as soon as the paste comes cleanly away from the sides of the bowl: if over-mixed, the pastry will become too elastic and doughy.

Wrap it in plastic and refrigerate for 30 minutes or overnight. Before using the pastry re-work it gently, taking care to keep it cold and firm.

On a lightly floured bench, roll the pastry out to about 3mm thick or as required for your recipe.

Store the unbaked pastry in the refrigerator or freezer, unfilled or filled. It is advisable to thaw it in the refrigerator overnight. Before rolling it out to its required thickness, let it stand at room temperature for approximately 30 minutes.

■ Makes enough pastry for 1 x 20cm round tart

Baking and Cooling

PRODUCT	TEMPERATURE	TIME
Unfilled short pastry	200–220°C	18–20 minutes
Filled short pastry	215–220°C	20–25 minutes
Unfilled sweet pastry	180–190°C	18–20 minutes
Filled sweet pastry	180–190°C	25–30 minutes
Cooked short and sweet pastry (to reheat)	180–190°C	15–25 minutes

Times and temperatures will vary from oven to oven.

■ Once the Short or Sweet Pastry is out of the oven it should be cooled on a rack to avoid sweating. Pies should be allowed to cool slightly before being removed from their tins to help the butter to set and to prevent the pie shell from collapsing.

How It Works

■ The mixing methods for Short and Sweet Pastry are designed to coat the flour particles with fat, preventing the protein (gluten) network from developing when the liquids are added. Mixing this way will always result in a tender pastry. This is achieved only with the correct mixing time: do not over-mix the pastry, or you will begin to develop the protein (gluten) network and the dough will become tough.

Keys to Success

■ Work in a cool environment.

■ Avoid excessive handling of the pastry.

■ Do not over-mix.

Choux Pastry

Before cooking, Choux Pastry is more like a batter than a firm dough or pastry. One of the prerequisites for top-quality choux pastries is cooking the roux base correctly. Another is knowing how much egg to add. There is only one method of producing Choux Pastry.

125ml water
75g butter
pinch of salt
105g bread flour
4 eggs (or as needed), beaten

■ Bring the water and butter to the boil in a saucepan. Remove from the heat, add the salt and flour, and return to a moderate heat. Cook this basic roux through for 4–5 minutes, stirring all the time. Remove from the heat when the mixture comes cleanly away from the sides of the pan.

Allow the roux to cool slightly. Add the eggs one at a time, beating well between each addition. Add enough egg to form 'soft peaks' or so that, when you run your finger through the mixture, trench walls remain standing for approximately 10 seconds before collapsing in on themselves. Place the mixture in a piping bag with a small piping tube inserted. Pipe onto a greased tray as required for your recipe. (Alternatively, you can spoon the mixture out onto the tray.) Bake immediately following the instructions below.

■ Makes 15-20 choux buns

Baking, Cooling and Storage

PRODUCT	TEMPERATURE	TIME
Choux pastry	220–225°C	20–25 minutes (includes 5 minutes' drying time)

Times and temperatures will vary from oven to oven.

■ Bake in a hot oven. Do not open the oven door for the first 15–20 minutes. Remove from the oven when the pastry is dry.

Place the baked Choux Pastry on a cooling rack. This will allow air circulation and prevent sweating. Fill as required once the pastry is cool.

It is common practice to freeze baked Choux Pastry and thaw it before use. Some bakers place the thawed baked pastry in a warm oven for a few minutes to eliminate any moisture from its time in the freezer.

How It Works

■ The Choux Pastry enters the oven as a thick, shiny mass. Once the moisture in the batter produces steam, it pushes upwards, causing the pastry to 'balloon' and rise. (Do not be tempted to open the oven at this stage.) Once the pastry has risen to its maximum and the moisture from the batter has escaped, the protein (albumen) in the eggs will coagulate (set), giving the pastry strength and structure to support the outer shell. This prevents a collapse during cooling.

Keys to Success

■ Do not over-cook the roux on the stove, as this will dry it out.

■ Always use fresh eggs. Fresh egg white is stronger, enhancing the pastry structure.

■ The quantity of egg used depends on the consistency of the mixture.

■ Always bake in a hot oven.

■ Never open the oven door too early, as this will allow the steam to escape, causing the Choux Pastry to collapse.

Choux pastry ready to be piped; note the consistency of the batter.

Best-Ever Bacon and Egg Pie

A perennial favourite for summer meals — especially picnics — this tasty bacon and egg pie is bursting with savoury aromas and tastes. It's perfect served warm or cold with a glass of chilled lager.

Butter Puff Pastry

■ Use one quantity of the Butter Puff Pastry on page 12. Make it a day ahead and store in the refrigerator, in plastic wrap.

Divide the pastry into two pieces, one slightly larger than the other. On a floured bench, roll the larger piece out and ease it into a fluted pie or flan tin with a removable base.

Bacon and Egg Filling

50g tasty cheese
6 thick slices bacon, rind removed
9 eggs
5 tablespoons chopped fresh parsley and basil
salt and freshly ground pepper
2 large tomatoes, firm but ripe

■ Use as directed below.

Assembly and Baking

1 egg, for sealing and glazing

■ Place a baking tray on the lower shelf of the oven and preheat to 210°C at this point, if your time is limited. For best results, however, the assembled pie should be rested for 1 hour before baking. If you plan to rest the pie, you can preheat the oven then.

Grate the cheese finely and scatter it over the pastry-lined base. Cut the bacon into small strips and place them in an even layer over the cheese. One at a time, break the eggs for the filling and carefully pour each onto the bacon. Try not to break the yolks.

Chop the herbs very finely and scatter them evenly over the eggs. Season liberally with salt and pepper. Slice the tomatoes thinly and place them on top.

Roll the remaining pastry out into a circle and cover the pie, reserving some pastry scraps. Break the remaining egg into a cup and beat it with a fork. Use a little of the beaten egg to seal the top pastry to the base by brushing the underside of the top pastry with egg and gently pressing it to the sides. Decorate the top of the pie with the leftover pastry. Brush the remaining beaten egg evenly over the top of the pie as a glaze.

If resting the pie for 1 hour before baking, preheat the oven and baking tray to 210°C at this point. Otherwise, place the pie on the hot baking tray and bake for 45–50 minutes until the pastry is golden-brown and crisp. Remove from the oven and allow to stand for at least 20 minutes before removing from the tin.

■ Makes 1 x 24cm round pie

Keys to Success

■ *Making the Butter Puff Pastry a day ahead will minimise shrinkage in the baked pie.*

■ *This pie can be made a day ahead and stored unbaked in the refrigerator.*

■ *Top-quality bacon will result in an excellent flavour.*

■ *Preheating the baking tray will help to bake the base.*

■ *Using a lower shelf of your oven will result in the pie baking more evenly, particularly on the base.*

Sour Cherry Pie

A flavoursome pie with a yeasted crust, as often found in Austria, Germany and the Benelux Countries. Most tart recipes call for the pastry to be made first, but in this case you make the filling first. The pastry must be used almost straight away because of the yeast action.

Sour Cherry Filling

2 x 425g cans sour cherries, stones removed
1 vanilla pod, cut lengthways
15g cornflour

■ Open the cans of cherries and strain the juice into a bowl. Reserve the cherries in a separate bowl. Pour 150ml of the cherry juice into a small saucepan. Scrape the vanilla pod seeds into the pan and add the pod. In a small bowl, make a slurry by mixing the cornflour with 2 tablespoons of cherry juice from the original bowl.

Bring the juice in the saucepan to the boil. Remove from the heat and add the cherry slurry. Whisk the mixture and return to a moderate heat for 2 minutes to thicken, stirring all the time. Remove the pan from the heat again and stir in the cherries. Pour the filling into a bowl, remove the pod and cover with plastic wrap. Cool until required.

Yeast Ferment

75ml water
15g fresh yeast (5g active dry yeast)
75g standard flour
1½ teaspoons sugar

■ Place the water and yeast in a bowl and whisk to dissolve the yeast. Add the flour and sugar and stir vigorously to make a paste. Set aside for 20 minutes to ferment.

Dough

150g standard flour
¼ teaspoon salt
1 small egg
1½ teaspoons sugar
90g butter, softened
Yeast Ferment

■ Mix all the ingredients until they form a well-combined and smooth dough. Do not over-mix, as this will cause shrinkage during rolling out and baking. Measure the dough into 250g for the base and 150g for the trellis top. Roll into round balls and cover with plastic wrap. Set aside on a floured bench for 10 minutes to rest.

On a lightly floured bench, roll the dough for the base out to 5mm thick. Place it in a greased, fluted flan tin with a removable base. Trim the edge of the pastry with a sharp knife.

Assembly and Baking

1 egg
2 tablespoons water
1–2 tablespoons granulated or raw sugar
icing sugar, for dusting

■ Pour the Sour Cherry Filling into the pastry base.

On a lightly floured bench, roll the top pastry out to 4mm thick. Using a sharp knife, cut strips 5mm wide and lay these on the pie in a trellis pattern. (Or roll, cut and stretch if using a trellis pastry-cutter.)

Rest the tart for 20–30 minutes, to allow the dough to ferment and rise. Meanwhile, preheat the oven to 220ºC.

Mix the egg and water together to make an egg-wash. Using a pastry brush, lightly egg-wash the trellis and sprinkle with the granulated sugar. Place the pie on a lower shelf of the oven and bake for 20 minutes. Remove from the oven, cool and dust with icing sugar before serving.

■ Makes 1 x 20cm round tart

Keys to Success

■ Feel free to change the fruits to suit your taste; there is an amazing array of exotic canned fruits in supermarkets.

■ Make the filling first – the day before if desired (store it in the refrigerator).

■ When you stir the cherries into the filling mixture, it is fine to break some of them up as this will enhance the texture.

■ Take care not to make the pastry too far in advance. If you have done this by mistake, cover it with plastic wrap and place it in the refrigerator to slow down the action of the yeast.

■ You can use a trellis pastry-cutter from a specialty shop to achieve the professional look.

■ To prevent the top of the pie from becoming too dark, place a sheet of baking paper on it after 15 minutes of baking.

French Apple Compote Pies

These divine little individual apple pies are inspired by the range of apple tarts that can be found in every good French pâtisserie. The buttery filling, topped with a thin slice of apple, is set in a light, crisp pastry. Wonderful served warm with cream or melt-in-the-mouth vanilla-bean ice-cream.

Short Pastry

■ Use one quantity of the Short Pastry on page 14 (for a sweeter result, substitute Sweet Pastry). Make it a day ahead, cover in plastic wrap and store in the refrigerator.

On a lightly floured bench, roll the short pastry out to 3mm thick. Cut seven 10cm circles (slightly larger than the muffin pans in which they will be baked). Line the muffin pans with the pastry circles so that the pastry reaches the top of each pan.

For the top pie-lids, roll the pastry out to 2mm thick and cut seven 6.5cm circles (to fit the diameter of the muffin pans).

Apple Compote Filling

60g butter
30g caster sugar
4 medium cooking apples, peeled, cored
    and cut into 5mm cubes
juice of ¼ lemon
100ml water
few drops pure vanilla essence
½ teaspoon ground cinnamon

■ Heat the butter and sugar in a heavy-based saucepan over a moderate heat until the butter is melted and the sugar lightly coloured. Add the apple cubes and sauté for 2 minutes. Add the lemon juice, water, vanilla and cinnamon.

Bring to the boil and simmer for 5 minutes, stirring occasionally, until the water has evaporated.

Place in a bowl to cool and cover with plastic wrap.

Assembly and Baking

75ml hot water
75g sugar
1 egg
2 tablespoons water
1 medium cooking apple (do not peel or core)

■ Preheat the oven to 190°C. Place the water and sugar in a small saucepan and boil to dissolve the sugar. Place the sugar syrup in a bowl until required.

Fill each pie almost to the top with Apple Compote Filling. Moisten the edges of the piecrusts, place the pastry lids on them and seal.

Mix the egg and water together to make an egg wash. Using a pastry brush, lightly egg-wash the pastry lids and slit a small hole in each.

Cut seven slices of apple 1–2mm thick, right through the centre (including the core). Dip each slice into the prepared sugar solution. Place an apple slice on top of each pastry lid, pressing down slightly to ensure the surfaces stick together. Bake the pies for 20–25 minutes until the pastry cases are golden-brown and the apple slices have started to caramelise. Remove from the oven and cool slightly before removing from the muffin pan.

■ Makes 7 muffin-sized pies

Keys to Success

■ *When rolling out the pastry lids, ensure they are not too thick; otherwise they will not bake properly.*

■ *Granny Smith apples are perfect for the filling.*

■ *The Apple Compote Filling can be made a day ahead and refrigerated, but return it to room temperature before using.*

Chicken, Camembert and Cranberry Pies

Savoury pies are one of the best New Zealand food traditions. Filled with beef chunks or mince, pies have been wolfed down in their millions. In recent years, with a wide range of tasty options becoming available, pie-munchers have indulged in gourmet pies. So here's a true gourmet pie at its best!

Butter Puff Pastry

■ Use one quantity of the Butter Puff Pastry on page 12. Make it a day ahead and store in the refrigerator, in plastic wrap.

If making one large pie, follow the pastry handling directions for the Best-Ever Bacon and Egg Pie on page 18.

Cut off a quarter of the pastry block and set it aside for the pie-lids. On a lightly floured bench, roll the remaining pastry out to a square 4mm thick. Cut into quarters. Line each individual greased pie tin with pastry, ensuring it is firm against the sides of the tins. Leave the pastry hanging over the edges.

Roll the smaller piece of pastry out to a square 3mm thick. Cut the square into quarters, cover with plastic wrap and set aside.

Chicken Filling

1 tablespoon olive oil
1 clove garlic, peeled and diced
250g chicken breast, skinned and diced

■ In a frying pan, heat the oil and sauté the garlic gently. Add the chicken and sauté for 5–7 minutes until cooked. Drain any excess juices and set aside for use in the Spiced Roux Sauce below.

Keys to Success

■ *The Chicken Filling and Spiced Roux Sauce can be made a day ahead and stored in the refrigerator.*

■ *For best results, make the pastry and filling the day before, then assemble at least 2–3 hours before baking. The longer the rest before baking, the less the pastry will shrink.*

■ *Make sure you roll the pastry out in a cool environment; otherwise the butter will become too soft and difficult to handle.*

Spiced Roux Sauce

50g butter
50g standard flour
300ml milk
Chicken Filling
1 teaspoon mustard seeds
¼ teaspoon freshly cracked black pepper
½ teaspoon salt
¼ teaspoon freshly ground nutmeg
1 teaspoon mixed herbs

■ In a saucepan, melt the butter over a moderate heat. Add the flour. Combine the two to form a firm paste. Slowly add a little milk and mix in thoroughly. Keep adding small quantities of milk, mixing each addition in thoroughly to prevent lumps from forming. A runny roux sauce will result. Stir in the Chicken Filling, mustard seeds, pepper, salt, nutmeg and herbs. Cover and set aside until required.

Assembly and Baking

2½ tablespoons store-bought cranberry sauce
4 slices camembert cheese
1 egg
2 tablespoons water
2 tablespoons sesame seeds

■ Fill each pastry-lined dish almost to the top with the Spiced Roux Sauce. Add 2 teaspoons of cranberry sauce to each and place a slice of camembert on top.

Brush the edges of the pastry bases with a little water and place the lids on top. Seal and trim excess pastry off with a sharp knife.

Mix the egg and water together to make an egg wash. Using a pastry brush, lightly egg-wash the top of each pie and sprinkle with sesame seeds.

Rest the pies for 1–2 hours (or longer) before baking. Preheat the oven to 220°C when appropriate. Bake the pies for 25–30 minutes. Remove from the oven and allow to cool in the tins for 10 minutes. Remove from the tins and place on a cooling rack.

■ Makes 4 individual pies or 1 x 24cm round pie

Sweet Potato, Feta, Tomato and Basil Pastries

Dean first came across these flavoursome pastries in a Notting Hill bakery in London. The versions made there used a Danish pastry that was too sweet for his taste. So we've adapted the recipe, using Butter Puff Pastry instead. It's perfect for a summer lunch, served with a fresh simple green salad.

Butter Puff Pastry

■ Use one quantity of the Butter Puff Pastry on page 12. Make it a day ahead and store in the refrigerator, in plastic wrap.

On a floured bench, roll the pastry out to a 40cm x 30cm rectangle 3-4mm thick. Mark the pastry into 10cm squares and cut these out using a sharp knife, so you end up with 12 squares. Cut 7cm-diameter circles in the middle of six squares. Discard the central circles or store in the freezer, in plastic wrap, for future use.

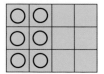

Savoury–Sweet Filling

*1 large sweet potato (preferably golden),
  peeled and cut into 1cm cubes
1 clove garlic, finely chopped
¼ small red onion, finely chopped
olive oil
¼ teaspoon fresh thyme
100g feta, cut into 1cm cubes
handful fresh basil
12 cherry tomatoes, halved
salt and freshly ground black pepper*

■ Preheat the oven to 180°C. Place the sweet potato, garlic and onion in a small roasting pan. Toss with the oil and thyme. Bake until the sweet potato becomes soft. Remove and cool until required.

Use the remaining filling ingredients as directed in the Assembly and Baking section below.

Assembly and Baking

*1 egg
2 tablespoons water
sesame seeds (optional)*

■ Mix the egg and water together to make an egg wash and glaze. Using a pastry brush, egg-wash the surfaces of the six complete pastry squares.

Lay the squares with the holes in them on top to make two layers of pastry, like a large, square vol-au-vent. Egg-wash the top surface of the pastry and sprinkle it lightly with sesame seeds, if using. An alternative to the sesame decoration is to score lines across the top pastry surface, using the back of a knife.

Place on a baking tray lined with baking paper and prick the bottom pastry (inside the hole) with a fork several times.

Into each pastry place 1½–2 heaped tablespoons of the cooked sweet potato mixture, 3–4 feta cubes and some sliced basil leaves (reserving 6 young sprigs for decoration). Top with cherry tomato halves. Drizzle with a little olive oil and season with salt and pepper.

Preheat the oven to 210°C while you set the pastries aside for at least 30 minutes. Bake for 15 minutes or until the pastry is puffed up and golden-brown. Remove from the oven. Serve warm or cool, garnished with sprigs of young basil.

■ Makes 6 pastries, each about 10cm square

Keys to Success

■ When rolling the puff pastry out to its final thickness, remember to allow it to relax and rest. This will make it easier to roll out and minimise shrinkage during baking.

■ You can make the pastry cases several hours in advance and keep them covered in the refrigerator until required.

■ Allow the pastries to rest for at least 30 minutes before baking.

■ A hot oven will result in an evenly risen puff pastry.

Portuguese Custard Tarts

These small, sweet versions of the traditional custard tart have spread from the Iberian Peninsula throughout Asia, where they have become a cult food. With their crisp, almost caramelised puff pastry cases, they are heavenly when eaten freshly baked and slightly warm.

Butter Puff Pastry

half quantity Butter Puff Pastry (recipe page 12)
2 teaspoons caster sugar

■ Make the pastry a day ahead and store in the refrigerator, in plastic wrap. You can make the full recipe and store the leftover pastry in the freezer, in plastic wrap, for future use.

On a floured bench, roll the pastry out to 3mm thick and a 24cm x 24cm square. Cut it in half. Brush one side very lightly with water, then sprinkle it with the sugar. Place the other pastry sheet on top of the sugar. Roll the rolling pin gently over the top pastry sheet to press the two sheets together.

Brush the surface lightly with water and roll the pastry up tightly from the 12cm end. Using a sharp knife, cut the log into 12 rounds, each 1cm. Place each round, one at a time, onto a lightly floured bench. Roll each round out to a circle of 10cm.

Press each pastry disc into lightly greased muffin pans. Ease the pastry gently down into the bottom, ensuring it fits into the corners of the pans. Set aside in the refrigerator to rest for at least 1 hour (the longer the better), to prevent shrinkage during baking.

Custard

165g caster sugar
70ml water
2 tablespoons cornflour
1½ tablespoons custard powder
500ml milk
4 egg yolks
½ teaspoon pure vanilla essence

■ Preheat the oven to 220ºC to prepare for the Assembly and Baking section below.

Place the sugar and water in a medium-sized saucepan on a low heat. Stir until the sugar dissolves, then remove from the heat.

In a bowl, combine the cornflour and custard powder. Gradually whisk in the milk until smooth, then whisk in the egg yolks.

Add the custard mixture to the saucepan with the sugar syrup. Cook over a moderate heat, stirring all the time until it thickens (3–4 minutes). Remove from the heat, stir in the vanilla and cover with plastic wrap. Allow to cool for 10 minutes before you assemble and bake the tarts.

Assembly and Baking

■ Put the custard into a jug for ease of pouring, then pour evenly into the pastry cases. Bake at 220ºC for 20–25 minutes or until the custard has set and the top has developed brown spots. The pastry should be crisp. Allow to cool slightly in the pans before removing, then transfer to a cooling rack.

■ Makes 12 muffin-sized tarts

Keys to Success

■ *When brushing water onto the pastry as described, don't use too much as this will cause problems when you handle the pastry.*

■ *Make sure you roll the pastry out in a cool environment, otherwise the butter will become too soft and difficult to handle.*

■ *A hot oven will result in a crisp puff pastry.*

■ *To achieve the spotted appearance on the surface of the custard, place the tarts under the grill for 2–3 minutes. Otherwise, if you have a gas blow-torch, gently dust the tops with icing sugar and caramelise with the blow-torch.*

Rhubarb, Cherry and Chocolate Tart

The intense flavours of this tart's sour cherries and rhubarb and its sweet, dark chocolate filling make a great combination. It's fantastic served warm with honey-and-vanilla-flavoured mascarpone and a cherry sauce. This recipe is a favourite of Marcus Braun, a bakery and pâtisserie teacher at the New Zealand Baking Training Centre.

Sweet Pastry

■ Use one quantity of the Sweet Pastry on page 14. Make it a day ahead and store in the refrigerator, in plastic wrap.

On a lightly floured bench, roll the pastry out to 3–4mm thick. Place it in a greased, fluted flan ring or rectangular tart tin with a removable base. Trim the edge with a sharp knife.

Cherry Sauce

1 x 425g can sour cherries, stones removed
2 tablespoons lemon juice
35g sugar
2 teaspoons cornflour
2 tablespoons cold water

■ Measure out 180ml of cherry juice from the can, reserving 120g of cherries for the Assembly and Baking section below.

Place the cherry juice, lemon juice and sugar in a saucepan and bring to the boil, stirring. In a small cup, dissolve the cornflour in the water. Add this slurry to the boiling juice and whisk constantly until the sauce thickens, approximately 1 minute. Pour into a bowl and cool before using.

Dark Chocolate Filling

125g butter, softened
3 egg yolks
zest of 1 orange
125g dark chocolate
3 egg whites
25g caster sugar
50g standard flour

■ Preheat the oven to 180°C to prepare for the Assembly and Baking section below.

Beat the butter, egg yolks and orange zest together until fluffy and creamy. Melt the chocolate in a bowl over very hot water. Slowly add the melted chocolate to the butter mixture and whisk until the two are well combined.

In a separate clean, grease-free bowl, whisk the egg whites to soft peaks. Slowly add the sugar in two or three stages. Gently fold half the egg whites into the chocolate-butter mixture. Sift in the flour. Fold it into the mixture with the remaining egg whites to achieve a smooth batter.

Assembly and Baking

120g sour cherries, reserved from the Cherry Sauce
140g rhubarb, peeled and chopped
dark chocolate or icing sugar

■ Distribute the cherries and rhubarb evenly over the base of the tart. Spread the Dark Chocolate Filling over the cherries and rhubarb with the back of a spoon, until level.

Bake at 180°C for 30–40 minutes until the filling is set. Remove from the oven and cool. Remove from the tin and sprinkle the top with dark chocolate curls or dust with icing sugar.

Serve with the Cherry Sauce and honey-and-vanilla-flavoured mascarpone or whipped cream.

■ Makes 1 x 24cm round or 11cm x 35cm rectangular tart

Keys to Success

■ Make the Cherry Sauce in advance to allow it to cool. You can heat it up in the microwave if you want to serve it warm.

■ If the tart is becoming too dark in the oven and it appears not to be completely set, put a sheet of baking paper over the top while the cooking continues.

French Caramel Walnut Tartlets

These little treats are a typical French tartlet and are great eaten freshly baked with a simple vanilla ice-cream. The Frangipane (almond cream filling) complements the caramel walnuts.

Sweet Pastry

■ Use half the quantity of the Sweet Pastry on page 14. Make it a day ahead and store in the refrigerator, in plastic wrap. You can make the full recipe, use what you need and store the rest in the freezer, in plastic wrap.

On a lightly floured bench, roll the pastry out to approximately 3mm thick. Cut circles slightly larger than the baking tins (approximately 10cm in diameter for an 8.5cm tin). Line the tins with pastry and trim the edge with a sharp knife.

Frangipane

50g butter, softened
50g sugar
1 egg, at room temperature
50g ground almonds
10g standard or bread flour

■ Using a wooden spoon, cream the butter and sugar until light and fluffy. Add the egg slowly, to prevent curdling, and beat to incorporate. Add the ground almonds and flour. Mix for a few minutes to achieve a smooth, creamy consistency.

Assembly and Baking

75 150ml cream
120g sugar
110g walnuts, roughly chopped

■ Preheat the oven to 200ºC. Fill each unbaked shell approximately a quarter full with Frangipane. Bake for about 15 minutes until lightly golden-brown.

Remove from the oven and cool. Tip the pastry shells out of the tart tins. Meanwhile, make a caramel walnut topping.

Heat the cream to boiling point, preferably by microwaving it for 30 seconds on high. At the same time, caramelise the sugar in a heavy-based saucepan on a moderate heat, without adding any water. Stir the sugar gently and continuously to prevent it from catching and burning.

As soon as the sugar turns amber, remove the saucepan from the heat. Gradually add the hot cream, stirring all the time to achieve a smooth, creamy caramel. Add the walnuts and stir. Add the topping to the pastry shells immediately, taking care not to overfill them.

■ Makes 6 x 8.5cm tarts

Keys to Success

■ *Always use top-quality fresh walnuts, preferably bought still in their shells. Packaged, shelled walnuts quickly turn bitter and rancid.*

■ *Take care that the cream is hot when adding it to the caramelised sugar. Cold cream will result in a lumpy caramel.*

■ *If the caramel hardens before use, re-warm it over a very low heat.*

■ *When making a 'dry' caramel, cook the sugar slowly and stir all the time to ensure it doesn't burn.*

Chocolate, Vanilla and Pear Custard Tart

This tart is a variation on the traditional chocolate and pear tart, which is generally based on an almond cream with cocoa powder added. Here, Dean has replaced that filling with custard and used real vanilla, pears and chocolate.

Sweet Pastry

■ Use one quantity of the Sweet Pastry on page 14. Make it a day ahead and store in the refrigerator, in plastic wrap.

On a lightly floured bench, roll the pastry out to 3–4mm thick, to fit inside a greased 20cm fluted flan ring or tart tin with a removable base. Line the tin with pastry and trim the edge with a sharp knife.

Vanilla Custard

1 egg
1 egg yolk
100ml cream
⅛ teaspoon ground nutmeg
½ teaspoon pure vanilla essence

■ Whisk together all the ingredients until they are well combined into a smooth liquid. Strain through a sieve into a pouring jug, then set aside.

Assembly and Baking

50g dark chocolate, grated
3 large pears, firm but ripe
3 tablespoons caster sugar
4 tablespoons water
100g apricot jam

■ Preheat the oven to 200°C. Sprinkle the bottom of the pastry case with the chocolate.

Peel, halve and core the pears. Cut thin slices crosswise almost to the base, keeping the halves intact. Fan them out slightly. Slipping a palette knife or metal spatula under the fanned-out pears, transfer each half onto the chocolate, arranging them like the spokes of a wheel.

Pour the Vanilla Custard evenly into the tart shell, avoiding the pears. Sprinkle the sugar evenly over the entire filling.

Carefully place the tart in the oven and bake for 10 minutes. Reduce the heat to 180°C and bake for approximately a further 20 minutes, while making the glaze below. Remove the tart from the oven when the custard is set and the pears are beginning to caramelise.

Put the water and jam in a saucepan and bring to the boil, stirring. Remove from the heat, strain through a sieve and brush onto the tart while still hot. Serve the tart warm or chilled.

■ Makes 1 x 20cm round tart

Keys to Success

■ *Make sure you use top-quality chocolate as this will improve the flavour. For a change, use white chocolate instead of the dark variety.*

■ *The custard can be made some hours in advance and refrigerated, but bring it to room temperature and stir before use.*

■ *Take care when filling the tart that you don't pour custard over the sliced pears. Otherwise they will not caramelise and the visual effect will be spoiled.*

Raisin–Rosemary Rice Pudding Tart

This recipe was inspired when Dean was in Germany during the cold winter months. A favourite fruit there is sour cherries; however, to make this an everyday tart, he has substituted plump golden raisins, a hint of rosemary and — for summer — added a topping of fresh berries. This tart has so many textures and taste sensations, it will be an instant hit.

Sweet Pastry

■ Use one quantity of the Sweet Pastry on page 14. Make it a day ahead and store in the refrigerator, in plastic wrap.

On a lightly floured bench, roll the pastry out to 3–4mm thick, to fit inside a greased 20cm fluted flan ring or tart tin with a removable base. Line the tin with pastry and trim the edge with a sharp knife. Place a circle of baking paper in the base, making sure it comes all the way up the sides of the tart case. Fill with baking beans or raw rice. Preheat the oven to 180°C while you set the pastry aside for at least 30 minutes to rest it.

Bake the pastry case blind for approximately 30 minutes or until golden-brown. Remove the paper and baking beans or raw rice and set the pastry aside to cool.

Rice Pudding Filling

1 vanilla pod, split
375ml full-cream milk
4 tablespoons arborio rice
2 tablespoons sugar
salt
1 large egg yolk
15g butter
¼ cup golden raisins, loosely packed
1 teaspoon fresh rosemary, roughly chopped

■ Scrape the vanilla pod seeds into the milk. Place the milk, vanilla pod, rice, sugar and salt in a heavy-based saucepan on a moderate heat. Bring to the boil, stirring occasionally. Reduce the heat to low.

Cook the rice pudding mixture, stirring constantly, until three-quarters of the milk has evaporated and the mixture has begun to thicken slightly. This should take 30–40 minutes. Remove from the heat when the rice is completely soft.

In a bowl, stir the egg yolk to break it up. Gradually stir in approximately 4 tablespoons of the cooked rice mixture, 1 tablespoon at a time. Return this enriched mixture to the rice pudding. Add the butter, raisins and rosemary and stir well to combine. Return the saucepan to a moderate heat, stir the pudding

vigorously and cook for a further 1–2 minutes or until a few bubbles pop on the surface. Do not boil.

Scrape the pudding into a clean bowl and cover with plastic wrap. Allow to cool at room temperature.

Assembly and Baking

400–500g fresh mixed berries
icing sugar, for dusting

■ Preheat the oven to 175°C. Remove all berry stems and discard. Wash the berries in cold water and dry on a paper towel.

Pour the Rice Pudding Filling into the baked pastry case. Using a spatula, spread the mixture evenly until it is level. Bake for 8–9 minutes, or 13–14 minutes if the mixture has just been removed from the refrigerator. Remove and allow to cool in the tin.

Remove from the tin and place on a serving plate. Arrange the berries on the top of the tart in a rustic fashion. Dust lightly with icing sugar just before serving.

■ Makes 1 x 20cm round tart

Keys to Success

■ *Choose plump golden raisins for best results.*

■ *The Rice Pudding Filling can be made a day ahead and refrigerated.*

■ *Strawberries, raspberries, blueberries, redcurrants and other berries can be used for the topping.*

■ *When cooking the rice mixture for the second time, take care not to boil it as this will curdle the egg yolk, making the filling unusable.*

Plum, Almond and Fennel Tart

The combination of contrasting but complementary flavours and textures is very pleasing and puts this dessert in a class of its own. Serve warm with vanilla-bean ice-cream.

Butter Puff Pastry

■ Use one quantity of the Butter Puff Pastry on page 12. Make it a day ahead and store in the refrigerator, in plastic wrap.

On a floured bench, roll the pastry out to approximately 4mm thick, to fit a greased 21cm-square fluted flan or tart tin with a removable base. Line the tin with pastry and trim the edge with a sharp knife.

Plum and Fennel Filling

10 red plums, skins on
½ cup sugar
1 tablespoon fennel seeds, lightly bruised

■ Wash and dry the plums. Cut each plum in half, remove the stone and cut the plum into quarters. Place in a bowl with the sugar and fennel seeds. Toss to coat the plums.

Cover the bowl with plastic wrap and leave the plums for 2–4 hours, tossing every so often to coat them again. Before using, reserve the syrup that has formed.

Almond Cream Filling

50g butter, softened
50g sugar
1 egg
50g ground almonds

■ Using a wooden spoon, cream the butter and sugar until light and fluffy. Add the egg slowly and beat until combined, then beat in the ground almonds. Cover and set aside until required.

Assembly and Baking

4 tablespoons water
100g apricot jam
icing sugar, if preferred

■ Coat the pastry base with a thin layer of the Almond Cream Filling. If using a square tart tin, arrange the plums in rows with the skin sides down and the flesh facing upwards on an almost vertical angle, until the tart is well packed with fruit. For a round tart, arrange the plums around the outside, then work inwards.

Drizzle the reserved fennel syrup evenly over the plums.

Leave the tart to rest for 20–30 minutes while you preheat the oven to 220°C. Bake for 25–30 minutes or until the fruit has turned dark at the edges.

To glaze the tart, put the water and jam in a saucepan and bring to the boil, stirring. Remove from the heat, strain through a sieve and brush over the fruit while both the tart and the glaze are hot.

Otherwise, sprinkle the tart with icing sugar just before serving.

■ Makes 1 x 21cm square or 20cm round tart

Keys to Success

■ *Making the Butter Puff Pastry a day ahead will minimise shrinkage in the baked tart.*

■ *This tart can be assembled a day ahead and stored unbaked in the refrigerator.*

■ *Place the tart in the lower part of the oven to ensure the base is well baked.*

■ *A hot oven will not only create a crisp pastry but will also caramelise the sugars within the plums, resulting in a pleasing dark-brown colour around the edges.*

breads

Making Bread

Making bread is one of the most relaxing and satisfying baking processes imaginable. Whether the results are soft and sweet, chewy and dense, light and crispy or chock-full of grains or fruits, much pleasure comes from taking the time and effort to create bread you can be proud of!

How It Works

■ Four independent ingredients — flour, water, salt and yeast — form a cohesive team to create bread. If the balance of ingredients is wrong, the teamwork goes awry.

Good bread flour contains a protein called gluten that gives structure and strength to all yeast-raised goods. To develop, gluten must absorb liquids. As the dough is kneaded, the gluten forms long, elastic and rubbery strands: the gluten network. High-fat and high-sugar doughs take less time to knead than other doughs, due to the effect these ingredients have on the gluten network.

The structure, nourishment, warmth and humidity help the yeast to break starches in the flour down into glucose and ferment them into carbon dioxide and alcohol. The gluten network captures the gas in tiny pockets or cells, causing the dough to inflate and expand in its bulk fermentation (first rising). The longer the dough is left to rise, the more fermentation occurs and the more alcohol is produced, giving a distinctive flavour to the resulting bread.

If the gluten network within the dough has not been correctly developed by kneading and if the dough has not been knocked back (pushed and folded) during the rising process, the carbon dioxide escapes. A collapsed, small-volume loaf results. Knocking back also revitalises the yeast's activity and makes the dough temperature consistent. It stimulates and strengthens the gluten network and evens out the cell structure.

The dough is rounded into balls, partly to ensure that the gas remains inside. A rest of 10–15 minutes relaxes the gluten network, then the dough is moulded into its final shape. The dough undergoes a final proof (second rising).

In baking, the unpalatable dough becomes a light, porous, digestible and flavoursome food. The baker sprays water or tosses ice cubes into the oven to create steam. The heat and moisture enable the yeast to lift the dough one last time (oven spring), the flour proteins set and the crust develops for the bread to gain its characteristic bloom (shine).

A Note on Bread-Making Machines

■ The concept of a bread-making machine is admirable: it introduces people to bread-making and makes the aroma and experience of just-baked bread available to all. However, those who develop an understanding of the philosophy and chemistry of baking will usually find that they want something more. That's where this book comes in: it offers hands-on experience of all the processes of bread-making, which in the end are rather more than pouring ingredients into a mould, adjusting a dial, flicking a switch and hoping for the best.

Bread-making machines can be used for the kneading process in this chapter's recipes. A word of warning, however: because bread-machine bakers don't have a hand (or two!) in the dough, they can't get a feeling for it. They can't constantly monitor it for wetness, softness, suppleness and those other subtle qualities that are so important. Without getting their hands sticky, they cannot know for certain whether the consistency of their dough is correct.

Measuring

■ Accuracy is particularly important when working with yeast-raised doughs. Where pinpoint accuracy is vital to the success of a recipe in this chapter, quantities have generally been given in weight rather than in teaspoons, cups or other measures that may vary from home to home and baker to baker. Quantities in weight are also preferable for those who want to bake recipes from the book on a larger scale than that specified.

Non-weight measurements have been used at times. Firstly, where accuracy is less crucial (as in some non-yeasted recipes or in glazing), a non-weight measurement may be simpler. Secondly, the quantity of a vital ingredient may be so small that domestic scales will not weigh it accurately (this is especially true of spices and active dry yeast, which are very light). Thirdly, liquids such as water and milk are the same in volume as in weight: for instance, 500ml of water is also 500g of water. The same does not apply to all other liquids, so please do not assume that you can always substitute measurements by volume for measurements by weight.

All teaspoon measurements in this chapter, and in the rest of the book, are based on level teaspoons.

Bakers should not need to make anything other than minor adjustments to quantities specified in this chapter; for instance, adding a small amount of water or flour to correct the dough consistency.

As a general guide, it should be noted that active dry yeast is used in approximately one-third the quantity of fresh yeast.

Weights given at the end of each recipe (e.g. 'Makes 1 x 1kg loaf') relate to the unbaked product.

Flour for dusting has not been measured or specified in this book's ingredient lists. It is assumed that all bakers worth their salt will have sufficient on hand!

Use a range of measuring spoons as an aid to accuracy in bread-making and other baking. A selection of bowls in various sizes will also prove invaluable to the home baker: this large mixing bowl is ideal for combining bread ingredients by hand.

Mixing and Kneading

■ Place the flour in a large bowl. Sprinkle the other dry ingredients around the edge of the flour.

■ Slowly pour the water and other liquids into the middle of the bowl of dry ingredients. Always keep a small amount of water back for adjusting the dough consistency.

■ Using a wooden spoon or your hand, mix the liquids in, using a circular motion. Stop when the ingredients have formed a firm dough.

■ Tip the dough onto a lightly floured bench ready for kneading. Have a small bowl of flour handy for dusting the bench during the kneading process.

■ Begin to knead the dough by the traditional hand method of pushing, folding the dough back on itself, turning it 90° and repeating this procedure. Adjust the dough consistency by adding more flour or water if necessary.

■ The whole kneading process should take about 15 minutes and result in a smooth, silky and elastic dough. Let the dough rest during the kneading process and you will find it will achieve this consistency more quickly.

■ An under-mixed or under-developed dough: when this dough is stretched out, it is rough and easily broken.

■ A correctly mixed dough: when stretched, it almost resembles a membrane.

Keys to Success

■ Kneading is one of the most important steps in bread-making. It is essential for a well-risen, airy loaf.

■ Ensure that you knead at a suitable height on a solid surface, with plenty of space.

■ The secret of easy and effective kneading by hand is to rest for 30-45 seconds several times during the kneading process. This allows both the baker and the elastic flour proteins to relax a little before further kneading.

■ Factors that determine when a dough is fully kneaded include the water temperature, the speed and style of kneading, and the selection and quantities of raw ingredients (doughs that are high in fat and sugar take less time to knead).

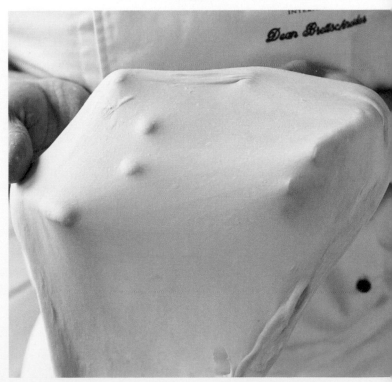

Other Pre-Baking Stages

Bulk Fermentation (also called First Rising)

■ The dough increases in volume during this stage, often to twice its original size. Bulk fermentation can take from 1–18 hours, depending on the levels of salt and yeast as well as the dough temperature, which should be 25–27°C.

Place the dough in a lightly oiled container large enough to allow it to double in size. Cover it to prevent the dough surface from skinning (forming a dry skin). Place the container in an environment where the temperature will remain constant.

About three-quarters of the way through bulk fermentation, the dough is knocked back. (This is also called 'punching down' but is more gentle than that term implies.) To knock back the dough, push and fold it very gently by hand. Return the dough to the container and cover it until needed for scaling.

Scaling and Rounding

■ Dough scaling or dividing takes place just after the dough has completed either its mixing or bulk fermentation stage. Divide the dough gently into the required sizes and weights.

After scaling, the dough pieces are rounded: shaped into smooth, round balls. Ensure the bench is flour-free. Cup your hands over the dough piece. With a little pressure, begin to move the dough in a circular motion, ensuring that it is touching the bench throughout. This movement stretches the surface of the dough so that it is completely smooth except for a seam where it has gripped the bench.

Intermediate Proof (also called First Proof, Recovery Time or Bench Time)

■ Cover the dough with plastic wrap, a dough cloth or a clean tea-towel to prevent the surface from skinning. Let the dough rest for 10-15 minutes.

Final Moulding and Placing

■ The specific details of moulding vary from recipe to recipe. They depend on practical considerations and any traditions that are associated with the bread variety being made. However, correct moulding is critical to the finished product.

All moulded bread doughs have a seam (see above in Scaling and Rounding). Place the dough seam-side down on trays and in tins, but seam-side up in cane proving baskets.

Apply toppings either at this point or after the final proof (see below in Cutting, Seeding and Dusting).

Moulding a round cob or boule.

Final Proof (also called Proving)

■ The proving temperature should be higher than the dough temperature; room temperature or 25°C is ideal.
Humidity is also needed at this stage. Without it, proving will slow down and skinning is likely. This formation of a dry skin on the dough prevents a glossy crust from forming during steaming and baking. Cover the dough loosely to retain the moisture, and use a spray bottle filled with warm water to prevent skinning.

Proving times depend on dough size, final dough temperature, yeast levels and even the ingredients used. It is common for a final proof to last 45–90 minutes in doughs that are not levain (sourdough) starter based.

Indentation Test

■ During the final proof, check whether the dough is ready for the next stage by pressing your finger lightly into the side of the dough.

The dough is under-proved if the pressed part quickly springs back to its original shape. It is correctly proved if the indentation mark reduces slowly but does not disappear.

The dough is over-proved if the dough collapses or the indentation mark does not move back at all. Put it in a correctly preheated oven as soon as possible, and be prepared for the resulting bread to be of inferior quality, with an open texture, little or no oven spring and pale in crust colours.

Cutting, Seeding and Dusting

■ These are the decorative parts of the process; optional extras that can make or break your bread in a beauty contest. Use a sharp knife or razor blade to cut or slash the dough, no later than three-quarters of the way through the final proof.

Sprinkle seeds on the dough just after moulding or just before you put the dough in the oven. If you do the latter, spray the dough lightly with water before you sprinkle the seeds, so they will stick to it. Grated cheese can also be applied at this stage.

Dusting the dough with flour at full proof allows the flour to bake onto the loaf or rolls.

Above left: Moulding baking-tray bread with pointed tapered ends, i.e. baton or baguettes.

Above: Moulding for a loaf tin.

Keys to Success

■ *The hot-water cupboard is one of the home baker's greatest assets. Use it to replicate the conditions of a commercial bakery in bulk fermentation and the final proof.*

■ *Rounding is one time you don't want a floured work-surface, as this will prevent the dough from gripping the bench.*

■ *Never under-estimate the importance of resting; allowing insufficient time for the intermediate proof will result in the dough tearing and becoming misshapen during final moulding.*

■ *The final proof requires close monitoring. Do the indentation test to check whether the dough is ready for its next stage.*

Baking, Cooling and Storage

PRODUCT	TEMPERATURE	TIME
Large dough pieces (400–500g)	220–230°C	30–40 minutes
Small dough pieces (100–200g)	200–210°C	12–18 minutes

■ The dough remains fragile and should be handled with care when being placed in the preheated oven.

Moisture is needed in the oven for the yeast to lift the dough one last time (oven spring). To create steam, home bakers can toss a few ice cubes into a preheated dish on a lower shelf of the oven. Alternatively, spray the sides of the oven and a baking stone with warm water 1 minute before putting the dough in to bake, and repeat this two or three times within the first 5 minutes of baking. Avoid spraying the heating elements and internal light fittings. Open the oven door narrowly to prevent steam and heat loss each time. Once the dough is in the oven, avoid spraying it directly with the water.

To check whether a loaf of bread is correctly baked, remove it from the oven and tap the base with your knuckles. If it sounds hollow, the loaf is ready to be removed from the oven.

As soon as you take loaves and rolls out of the oven, place them on a cooling rack and leave them to cool completely.

Breads to be served within 8 hours may be left uncovered or in a paper bag. Breads that are to retain a crust must not be packaged, as this will soften the crust. If you plan to freeze your bread, place it in a plastic bag for optimum storage. Never place bread into the refrigerator: this will make it go stale more quickly.

Keys to Success

■ The longer the baking time . . .
the thicker the crust;
the greater the moisture loss;
the darker the crust colour.

■ The higher the baking temperature . . .
the shorter the baking time;
the thinner the crust;
the greater the risk that larger dough pieces will under-bake and collapse.

■ The lower the baking temperature . . .
the longer the total baking time;
the thicker the product crust;
the more oven spring.

■ A cooling rack prevents loaves and rolls from sweating after baking.

■ Allow freshly baked bread to cool completely before slicing or cutting. This will enable you to cut evenly and show the texture at its full potential.

■ Flavour and aroma continue developing until the loaf has cooled completely – another reason to wait patiently before you devour it.

Dean's Pain au Levain, cut with his signature 'B' on the top.

White Sandwich Bread

The most basic bread has enduring popularity. Feel free to make it without a loaf tin and shape it into small rolls to serve at a dinner party.

300g bread flour
5g salt
5g sugar
10g fresh yeast (1 teaspoon active dry yeast)
10g olive oil
185ml water, warmed to 25°C
10g chilled butter, cut into 5mm cubes
3–4 ice cubes
melted butter, for glazing

■ Place all the ingredients except the butter and ice cubes in a bowl. Using a wooden spoon, combine them until a dough has formed. Tip the dough out onto a lightly floured bench. Knead for 15 minutes (resting every 3–4 minutes for 30 seconds) until the dough is smooth and elastic in consistency.

Lightly oil a bowl large enough to allow the dough to double in size. Put the dough in the bowl and cover it with plastic wrap. Leave in a warm place for 1 hour. Knock back the dough in the bowl by gently folding it back onto itself. Cover it again with plastic wrap and leave for a further 30 minutes.

Tip the dough out onto the bench, flatten it slightly and mould into a rectangular loaf shape. Place the dough in a greased loaf tin, cover it with plastic wrap and leave to prove for 1 hour. Meanwhile, place a small dish on the bottom shelf of the oven and preheat the oven to 200–210°C.

Using a sharp knife or razor blade, cut straight down the centre of the loaf lengthways, approximately 1cm deep. Place the butter cubes down the length of the cut.

Place the loaf tin in the oven, toss the ice cubes into the heated dish and quickly close the oven door. Bake for 20–25 minutes, until golden-brown. Remove the loaf from the oven and brush the surface immediately with the melted butter.

■ Makes 1 x 500g loaf

Keys to Success

■ *During kneading, the dough will initially be sticky to the touch. It's fine to add a little flour, if needed, but don't be tempted to add too much. Persevere with kneading until the dough is soft, smooth and supple.*

■ *Knocking back will deflate the dough slightly. It is important for strengthening the bread.*

■ *The lengthways cut is both for aesthetic purposes and to enable the top of the bread to rise evenly.*

■ *The ice cubes will create the steam needed for the flour proteins to set.*

■ *To make whole-wheat bread, simply use 150g bread flour (white) and 150g wholemeal flour.*

Basic Baguettes

A no-frills, no-fuss baguette recipe, less time-consuming than some. These loaves boast the crisp crust and airy centre for which French bread is famous. Best eaten very fresh!

300g bread flour
5g salt
5g sugar
10g fresh yeast (1 teaspoon active dry yeast)
185ml water, warmed to 25°C
3–4 ice cubes

■ Place all the ingredients except the ice cubes in a bowl. Using a wooden spoon, combine them until a dough has formed. Tip the dough out onto a lightly floured bench. Knead for 15 minutes (resting every 3–4 minutes for 30 seconds) until the dough is smooth and elastic in consistency.

Lightly oil a bowl large enough to allow the dough to double in size. Put the dough in the bowl and cover it with plastic wrap. Leave in a warm place for 1 hour. Knock back the dough in the bowl by gently folding it back onto itself. Cover it again with plastic wrap and leave for a further 30 minutes.

Tip the dough out onto the bench and divide it into three equal portions. Shape these into small rectangles and use your hands to roll them up into a tight Swiss roll. Roll the dough pieces out to small baguette shapes, each 25–30cm long with tapered ends. Place them on a baking tray lined with baking paper, cover with plastic wrap and leave to prove for 1–2 hours. Meanwhile, place a small dish on the bottom shelf of the oven and preheat the oven to 240°C.

Lightly dust the baguettes with flour. Using a sharp knife, make four shallow diagonal slashes across the top of each baguette.

Place the baking tray in the oven, toss the ice cubes into the heated dish and quickly close the oven door. Bake for 15 minutes. Turn the tray around and reduce the oven temperature to 200°C. Bake for a further 10 minutes or until the baguettes are dark golden-brown and the bases sound hollow when tapped.

■ Makes 3 x 165g baguettes or 2 longer loaves

Keys to Success

■ This is a basic French bread recipe that can be used to make more substantial boules (round loaves) as well as baguettes.

■ This dough is soft and a little sticky during kneading. Don't be tempted to add extra flour. The stickiness will disappear during the kneading and rising stages.

■ Knocking back will deflate the dough slightly. It is important for strengthening the bread dough.

■ Tossing ice cubes into a heated dish in the oven produces instant steam, enabling the dough to rise evenly.

■ In the unlikely event that you have baguettes left over, use them in the Chocolate, Rum and Raisin Bread Pudding recipe on page 96.

Levain Starter

Levain is a French word derived from the Latin levare: to rise. Dean's Pain au Levain (see page 82) is naturally leavened or sourdough bread. It relies on a starter: a bubbly, yeasty, batter-like substance that will give your bread its unique character, moist and open texture, tangy flavour and russet crust.

How It Works

■ Flour and water are combined, and yeast spores from various wild strains join the mixture from the fresh air around it. After the first 24 hours, bubbles may appear. These show that yeast has broken starches in the flour down into glucose, which it is fermenting into carbon dioxide and alcohol. The gas, trapped in the gluten network, will expand the mixture. Over the next four days, the yeast spores breed. They've been fed regularly but now they start getting through the food more quickly, so more frequent feeding is needed.

A week into the starter's life, the yeast has multiplied to just the right concentration. At this point your starter is like a new pet: it's established but needs ongoing care. By the tenth day, it is strong enough to bake with. As it matures, it develops further strength, consistency, balance and (to a certain extent) immunity.

If you refrigerate your starter, most of the yeast becomes dormant. But as time goes on it starts to die off, so occasional feeds are still needed. Warmth reactivates the yeast.

Day One

400g bread flour
500ml water, warmed to approximately 25°C

■ Mix the flour and water to a smooth batter in a large, preferably glass, bowl. This mixture is the basic culture for the recipe. Cover the bowl with muslin and leave for 24 hours.

Day Two

■ In the first 24 hours, some bubbles may have appeared on the surface. Use a wooden spoon to beat air into the mixture, cover the bowl with the muslin again and leave it for another 24 hours.

Sourdough rising in a linen-lined cane basket.

Days Three and Four

Per Feed:
200ml water, warmed to approximately 25°C
200g bread flour

■ Bubbles should be appearing on the surface now. On day three, pour the water into the bowl and break the culture up in it. Add the flour and mix well. Cover the bowl with the muslin again and let it stand in a warm place. Leave the culture about 24 hours before feeding it again on day four with water and flour.

Days Five and Six

Per Feed:
200ml water, warmed to approximately 25°C
200g bread flour

■ On day five, approximately 12 hours after feeding the starter on day four, discard half the culture. Feed the remainder of the culture as above. After another 12 hours, feed the culture again. On day six, repeat the activities of day five.

Day Seven Onwards

■ Feed the starter three times a day, allowing approximately eight hours' fermenting time between each feed. By day 10, it should be strong enough to make bread.

First Feed
100g starter (discard the rest)
50g bread flour
50ml water, warmed to approximately 25°C

Second Feed
200g starter (discard the rest)
100g bread flour
100ml water, warmed to approximately 25°C

Third Feed
400g starter (discard the rest)
200g bread flour
200ml water, warmed to approximately 25°C

Two Weeks Onwards

■ After a couple of weeks, if all has gone well, you should have a happy and healthy sourdough starter living in your home. With good care, it will last a very long time.

If you're going away, appoint a minder — or you can take your starter with you. Dean's starter has been known to accompany him on holiday!

Your ongoing feeding schedule can be organised to suit your day and your baking plans. Dean prefers to make his dough first thing in the morning, so he generally feeds the starter at 8am and 8pm on the day before baking (two feeds a day), making his dough at 8am the following day.

The feeding quantities for a starter once it is healthy vary from baker to baker. Here is a good guide: the formula should stay the same; the total weight of starter (which can vary) should be fed with half its quantity in water and half in flour. For example, 250g starter + 125ml water + 125g flour = 500g starter.

Low-Maintenance Mode

■ If you are maintaining your starter but not planning to make bread, discarding nearly 1kg of starter every day is quite wasteful — even if you share some of it with friends. Once your starter is bubbling along in a healthy way (at least two weeks after day one), you can slow development down by refrigerating it if you are not using it. Do this just after the first feed of the day.

The refrigerated starter will still need feeding occasionally. This can be done once a week. Use the same quantities of water and flour as above (discarding the excess starter as required), but warm the water to approximately 35°C.

At least two days before you plan to bake with the starter again, return it to room temperature and resume feeding three times a day. If you try to make bread with starter straight from the fridge, you will fail.

Keys to Success

■ *On days one and two, leave your starter where it will get plenty of fresh air but no direct sunlight. In winter, put it in the warmest part of the house and ensure it receives fresh air occasionally.*

■ *From day seven, transfer the starter to a container with a lid that has a small air-hole.*

■ *For consistent results, be consistent in your feeding schedule.*

■ *You can bake with the starter from about day 10.*

■ *The time taken to develop the Levain Starter is a major factor in the distinctive sourdough flavour: the lengthy fermentation process produces not only carbon dioxide but also alcohol.*

Baby Fig, Nut and Aniseed Loaves

These small loaves contain no dairy products but they're perfect served with cheese. They're deliciously chock-full of sweet figs and toasted almonds, and infused with the elegant scent of aniseed.

100g blanched almonds
150g dried figs (approximately 15)
500g bread flour
10g salt
10g olive oil
25g fresh yeast (8g active dry yeast)
350ml water, warmed to 25°C
20g whole aniseed, lightly bruised
3–4 ice cubes

■ Preheat the oven to 150°C. Toast the almonds on a baking tray until they are light brown in colour, approximately 10 minutes. Cool and chop roughly. To prepare the figs, remove the hard stems and cut each fig into five or six pieces.

Place the flour, salt, oil and yeast in a bowl and mix. Add the water. Using a wooden spoon, combine the ingredients to form a dough. Tip the dough out onto a lightly floured bench and knead for 10–15 minutes (resting every 3–4 minutes for 30 seconds) until the dough is smooth and elastic in consistency. During the last 2 minutes, add the aniseed and knead until well incorporated. Add the figs and almonds, kneading gently to incorporate them evenly. Take care not to break up the figs too much.

Put the dough in a lightly oiled bowl and cover it with plastic wrap. Leave in a warm place until the dough has almost doubled in size, approximately 45 minutes.

Tip the dough out onto the bench and give it a knock back by gently folding it onto itself three or four times. Return it to the bowl and cover with plastic wrap. Leave in a warm place for a further 30 minutes.

Gently tip the dough onto the bench and divide it into five equal portions (approximately 225g each). Shape each piece of dough into a small rectangle and roll up into a tight Swiss roll with tapered ends. Place them on a baking tray lined with baking paper; cover with plastic wrap and leave to prove for approximately 45 minutes. Meanwhile, place a small dish on the bottom shelf of the oven and preheat the oven to 230°C.

Using a sharp knife, make three shallow diagonal slashes across the top of each loaf. Place the baking tray in the oven, toss the ice cubes into the heated dish and quickly close the oven door.

Bake the loaves for 15 minutes. Turn the tray around and reduce the oven temperature to 200°C. Bake for a further 10 minutes or until the loaves are dark golden-brown and the bases sound hollow when tapped. Remove from the oven and cool on a rack.

■ Makes 5 x 225g loaves

Keys to Success

■ *Use dried figs, not fresh dessert figs.*

■ *If you cannot get whole aniseed, use fennel seeds instead. Do not use star anise! (It's completely different from aniseed, and will be impossibly hard and crunchy if baked.)*

■ *To bruise the aniseed, place the seeds on a solid bench and roll them lightly with a rolling pin or use a pestle and mortar. This will release the flavour.*

■ *Bear in mind that nuts continue cooking and colouring after they come out of the oven, as they contain a high proportion of oil and are very dense.*

■ *Kneading the dough should not be hard work. Take your time; don't rush this process.*

■ *Throwing ice cubes into a heated dish in the oven produces instant steam that enables the dough to rise evenly.*

Garlic and Coriander Naan

A great treat with any spicy dish. These flat breads can be made in advance and reheated in the oven to revive their 'freshly baked' aroma. Tear the naan apart and sop up delicious curry juices with it.

280g bread flour
60g yoghurt
5g salt
10g honey
5g garlic, finely chopped (approximately 1 clove)
15g butter, melted
1 teaspoon ground coriander
15g fresh yeast (5g active dry yeast)
125ml water (or as needed)
1½ teaspoons onion seeds or nigella seeds
1 tablespoon fresh coriander, finely chopped
1 tablespoon butter, melted, for glazing

■ Place the flour, yoghurt, salt, honey, garlic, melted butter, ground coriander, yeast and water in a bowl. Mix until a firm dough has formed.

Tip the dough out onto a lightly floured bench and knead for 10–15 minutes (resting every 3–4 minutes for 30 seconds) until the dough is smooth and elastic in consistency. During the last 2 minutes of kneading, add the onion or nigella seeds and fresh coriander. Knead until well incorporated.

Put the dough in a lightly oiled large bowl and cover it with plastic wrap. Leave in a warm place for 30–45 minutes until the dough has almost doubled in size.

Divide the dough into four equal portions. Mould each into a ball, place on a floured bench and cover with plastic wrap. Leave to rise for a further 30 minutes.

Place a baking tray on the middle shelf of the oven and preheat the oven to 250°C. Roll each dough ball out on the bench to form a teardrop shape approximately 5mm thick. Cover with plastic wrap and leave to rise for a further 15–20 minutes.

Gently transfer two dough pieces to a cold baking tray lined with baking paper. Slide the baking paper, complete with dough, onto the preheated baking tray. Bake for 3–4 minutes, until the breads are puffed up with brown spots.

Remove the baked naan breads from the oven and brush with melted butter while they are still hot. Bake and brush the remaining dough pieces in the same way.

■ Makes 4 x 125g naan breads

Keys to Success

■ *Avoid the temptation of adding more garlic, as this will weaken and soften the flour proteins, making the dough too soft and sticky.*

■ *Setting the oven at its highest temperature, 250°C, will cause the dough to puff up and bubble, which is desirable in naan.*

■ *If you wish to use a baking stone instead of a baking tray, place this in the oven an hour before baking. A baking stone is ideal as it conducts heat well, dispersing it evenly.*

■ *Avoid baking too long as this will dry the naan breads out.*

■ *Brushing the breads with melted butter after baking will enhance their soft texture and buttery taste.*

Green Tea and Sultana Breakfast Loaf

For many years green tea has been regarded as having health-giving properties. The secret lies in its high levels of catechin polyphenol, a powerful antioxidant. Health-giving or not, this loaf is soft, sweet and subtly aromatic. And as a Chinese proverb tells us, 'Better to be deprived of food for three days, than tea for one'.

180ml green tea, prepared as below
300g bread flour
5g salt
25g butter
25g sugar
15g fresh yeast (5g active dry yeast)
50g egg (approximately 1 egg, broken
    then weighed)
110g plump sultanas
10g chilled butter, cut into 5mm cubes
3–4 ice cubes
20g butter, melted, for glazing

■ The day before you plan to bake this loaf, boil water for the tea and add five green tea-bags to it. Infuse until the water is lukewarm, then break the bags open and empty the tea leaves into the water. (Do not discard the leaves, as they should be baked in the loaf.) Set aside for 8–10 hours, preferably overnight.

Place the tea, flour, salt, butter, sugar, yeast and egg in a bowl. Using a wooden spoon, mix the ingredients until a dough has formed. Tip the dough out onto a lightly floured bench and knead for 15 minutes (resting every 3–4 minutes for 30 seconds) until the dough is smooth and elastic in consistency. Finally, add the sultanas and continue to knead very gently until they are incorporated.

Lightly oil a bowl large enough to allow the dough to double in size. Put the dough in the bowl and cover it with plastic wrap. Leave in a warm place for 45 minutes. Knock back the dough in the bowl by gently folding it back onto itself. Cover it again with plastic wrap and leave for a further 30 minutes.

Tip the dough out onto the bench and mould it into a rectangular loaf shape. Place the dough in a greased loaf tin, cover it with plastic wrap and leave to prove for approximately 1 hour. Meanwhile, place a small dish on the bottom shelf of the oven and preheat the oven to 190°C.

Using a sharp knife or razor blade, cut straight down the centre of the loaf lengthways, approximately 1cm deep. Place the butter cubes down the length of the cut.

Place the loaf tin on a lower shelf of the oven, toss the ice cubes into the heated dish and quickly close the oven door.

Bake for 20–25 minutes, until golden-brown. Remove the loaf from the oven and brush the surface immediately with the melted butter.

■ Makes 1 x 700g loaf

Keys to Success

■ *If you want to make the sultanas extra-plump, infuse them in 2 tablespoons of the green tea the day before baking.*

■ *When kneading the sultanas into the dough, do it gently to prevent them breaking up – especially if they have been infused in the green tea, which will make them more fragile.*

■ *Knocking back will deflate the dough slightly. It is important for strengthening the bread dough.*

■ *The sugar, butter and egg in this recipe make the dough very soft; it will also be a little sticky. Don't be tempted to add extra flour. The stickiness will disappear during the kneading process and the two rising stages.*

■ *The quantities of sugar, butter and egg also mean the loaf will brown relatively quickly. Don't bake at a hotter temperature than 190°C as the loaf will then become too dark.*

Red Onion Fougasse

An oldie but a goodie. The distinctive onion flavour and the visual appeal of the leaf shape make this flat bread just perfect to accompany any hearty soup, particularly French Onion Soup. All good bakeries should have this irresistible loaf in their repertoire — and for the home baker it's a tour de force!

'Day Before' Dough

60g bread flour
pinch of salt
½ teaspoon fresh yeast (⅛ teaspoon active
  dry yeast)
40ml water

■ Make this at least 12–16 hours before use.

Mix all the ingredients in a bowl to form a dough. Place the dough on a lightly floured bench and knead for 8–10 minutes until it is smooth and elastic in consistency. Lightly oil a bowl large enough to allow the dough to double in size. Put the dough in the bowl, cover it with plastic wrap and leave overnight to ferment.

Final Dough

250g bread flour
1 quantity 'Day Before' Dough
5g salt
10g fresh yeast (1 teaspoon active dry yeast)
10g olive oil
160ml warm water
75g red onions, finely chopped
water, for spraying
olive oil, for glazing (optional)

■ Place all the ingredients except the last three in a bowl. Using a wooden spoon, combine them until a dough has formed.

Tip the dough out onto a lightly floured bench and knead for 10–15 minutes (resting every 3–4 minutes for 30 seconds). Check frequently for stickiness. Add a little flour if necessary, but be aware that stickiness will reduce with kneading anyway.

Add the onions and continue to knead until they are fully incorporated. The dough should no longer be sticky; its consistency should be smooth and elastic.

Lightly oil a bowl large enough to allow the dough to double in size. Put the dough in the bowl and cover it with plastic wrap. Leave in a warm place for 1½ hours. Knock back the dough in the bowl by gently folding it back onto itself. Cover it again with plastic wrap and leave for a further 30 minutes.

Tip the dough out onto the bench. Using a dough scraper, cut the dough into three pieces, each weighing approximately 200g. Gently and loosely mould each dough piece into an oblong. Lay the pieces on the bench, cover them with plastic wrap and allow to rest for 15 minutes.

Roll each dough piece out on the bench to form ovals, approximately 15cm long by 10cm wide and 1cm thick. Using a sharp knife or dough scraper, cut two 5cm-long diagonal lines all the way through one dough piece on each side. Cut one 5cm-long line straight down the middle of the dough, again all the way through. Pull each cut apart so that gaping holes appear. Repeat with the remaining dough pieces.

Place the dough on baking trays lined with baking paper (one or two pieces per baking tray). Allow about 5cm between each piece and ensure that the gaping holes remain in each one. Cut a small nick in the top and pull apart. Cover the baking trays with plastic wrap and leave them in a warm place to prove for 30–35 minutes. Meanwhile, preheat the oven to 230–240°C.

Spray the dough pieces lightly with water and bake for 15–18 minutes until crisp and lightly golden. Remove from the oven, brush lightly with olive oil if desired and cool on a rack.

■ Makes 3 x 200g fougasses

Keys to Success

■ The lengthy fermentation of the 'Day Before' Dough enhances the bread's flavour and texture.

■ The dough will be slightly wet and sticky after the onions are added. Take your time kneading them in, and it will become workable again. If the dough is far too sticky because the onions are very wet, add a small amount of flour and knead in.

■ Make sure you spread the cuts in the dough wide open with your fingers after you have made them, otherwise they will close up during proving and baking. The objective is to have leaf-shaped loaves with gaping holes in them.

Onion and Bacon Flammkuchen

This pizza-style bread comes from the Alsace region of France, bordering Germany. There are many, many variations, but the traditional Alsace flammkuchen is made with a hefeteig (yeasted dough), spread with crème fraîche and topped with diced bacon and sliced onions. Here Dean has enhanced the flavour and colour, for flammkuchen is a very pale bread.

Dough

100g bread flour
½ teaspoon salt
15g olive oil
*½ teaspoon fresh yeast (⅛ teaspoon active
    dry yeast)*
60ml water, warmed to 25°C

■ Place all the ingredients in a bowl. Using a wooden spoon, combine them until a dough has formed.

Tip the dough out onto a lightly floured bench and knead for approximately 10 minutes (resting every 3–4 minutes for 30 seconds) until the dough is smooth and elastic in consistency.

Lightly oil a bowl large enough to allow the dough to double in size. Put the dough in the bowl and cover it with plastic wrap. Leave in a warm place for 45 minutes. Knock back the dough in the bowl by gently folding it back onto itself so that it has a round shape. Cover it again with plastic wrap and leave for a further 30 minutes.

Tip the dough out onto the bench and flatten it slightly with the palm of your hand. Roll the dough out to a circle 28cm in diameter. Place it on a baking tray lined with baking paper.

Topping

150g thick crème fraîche
1 small onion, sliced
70g bacon, diced
3 cherry tomatoes, sliced
small sprig fresh rosemary
salt and freshly ground black pepper
extra-virgin olive oil, for drizzling

■ Using the back of a tablespoon, spread a thick layer of the crème fraîche over the dough, right out towards the edge. Sprinkle with the onion and bacon. Space the tomato evenly across the topping and toss rosemary leaves over the whole flammkuchen. Season with salt and pepper, then drizzle lightly with olive oil.

Cover the flammkuchen loosely with aluminium foil and rest it for 20 minutes before baking. Meanwhile, place a second baking tray on a middle shelf of the oven and preheat the oven to 250°C.

Open the oven and carefully slide the flammkuchen and baking paper onto the preheated tray. Bake for approximately 10 minutes. Remove the aluminium foil and bake for a further 5 minutes. Serve hot.

■ Makes 1 x 28cm round flammkuchen

Keys to Success

■ *Soften the crème fraîche by stirring it with a spoon, before spreading it over the dough base.*

■ *Don't be too tempted to jazz up the topping. The simplicity is a key factor in its great taste.*

■ *The preheated baking tray will help make the base crisp. If you wish to use a baking stone instead of a baking tray, heat this in the oven an hour before baking.*

■ *The aluminium foil used for the first stage of baking will stop the crème fraîche from evaporating and the rest of the topping from drying out. Avoid over-baking, as this will dry out the flammkuchen's base as well as its topping.*

Chardonnay Loaf

Artistic and larger than life, this is a celebration loaf for a special occasion or gift. The combination of wine and flours (including wholemeal and rye) give it an unforgettable nutty, Chardonnay aroma. The bread's firm yet irregular texture makes it a great part of any meal, and it's amazing lightly toasted . . . well worth the effort!

Chardonnay Loaf 'Day Before' Starter

100g bread flour
pinch of salt
½ teaspoon fresh yeast (⅛ teaspoon active dry yeast)
60ml Chardonnay wine, warmed to 25°C

■ Place all the ingredients in a bowl, then mix them until a dough is formed. Tip the dough out onto a lightly floured bench and knead for 8–10 minutes, until the dough is smooth and elastic in consistency. Lightly oil a bowl large enough to allow the dough to double in size. Put the dough in the bowl and cover it with plastic wrap. Leave for at least 12–16 hours.

Decorating Dough

200g flour
¼ teaspoon salt
20g butter, softened
85ml water

■ Place all the ingredients in a bowl. Using a wooden spoon, combine them until a dough has formed. Tip the dough out onto a lightly floured bench and knead for 7–8 minutes. The dough should be firm, so don't be tempted to add more water. Cover it with plastic wrap and store until needed to decorate the Chardonnay Dough.

Chardonnay Dough

400g bread flour
50g wholemeal flour
50g rye flour
1 quantity Chardonnay Loaf 'Day Before' Starter
10g salt
15g fresh yeast (5g active dry yeast)
350ml lukewarm fruity Chardonnay wine, freshly opened

■ Place all the ingredients in a bowl. Using a wooden spoon, combine them until a dough has formed. Tip the dough out onto a lightly floured bench. Knead for 10–15 minutes (resting every 3–4 minutes for 30 seconds). Check frequently for stickiness; add a little flour if necessary, but be aware that stickiness will reduce with kneading anyway. Add water if necessary to make the dough soft rather than firm. Stop kneading when it is no longer sticky in consistency but smooth and elastic.

Lightly oil a bowl large enough to allow the dough to double in size. Place the dough in the bowl and cover it with plastic wrap. Leave in a warm place until bubbles are appearing and it has expanded, approximately 45 minutes. Knock back the dough in the bowl by gently folding it onto itself several times. Cover it again with plastic wrap and leave for a further 45 minutes.

Tip the dough out onto the bench and gently mould it into a ball by cupping your hands around it and moving them in a circular motion, easing and stretching the surface of the dough. Be very gentle or the surface will rip and the appearance of the finished loaf will be spoilt. The final shape will be smooth and round except for the base, which will be rough and scrunched up.

Place the dough with the scrunched-up seam facing down onto a baking tray lined with baking paper. Dust the loaf with flour and cover loosely with plastic wrap. Leave it in a warm, draft-free place for approximately 1½ hours.

Meanwhile, shape the Decorating Dough as directed in the Assembly and Baking section overleaf. Apply the decoration once the dough has fully risen.

Assembly and Baking

1 egg
2 tablespoons water
3–4 ice cubes

■ Place a small dish in the oven and preheat the oven to 230°C. Combine the egg and water to make an egg wash.

Use the Decorating Dough to create a bunch of grapes, making numerous small marble-sized balls and sticking them together with a little water. Cut out one or two large vine leaves and some slender vine strands.

Using a pastry brush and water, gently brush the part of the loaf to be covered with the decoration. Apply the grapes and leaves to the loaf, then egg-wash them.

Using a sharp knife or razor blade, gently cut a ring around the loaf, approximately ½cm deep, a quarter of the way up from the base.

Place the baking tray in the oven, toss the ice cubes into the heated dish and quickly close the oven door. Bake for 20 minutes, then turn the oven down to 200°C and bake for a further 20–25 minutes or until the base of the loaf sounds hollow when tapped. Remove from the oven and cool on a rack.

■ Makes 1 x 1.050kg loaf

Keys to Success

■ *Prepare the Decorating Dough in advance and store in plastic wrap until needed. It will keep for at least one day at room temperature or two days in the refrigerator (return to room temperature in time for it to be moulded easily).*

■ *Instead of making a bunch of grapes, try a sheaf of wheat – or let your artistic imagination run wild!*

■ *If the decoration is becoming dark in the oven but the loaf is still not baked, reduce the temperature to 200°C and place a piece of baking paper over the decoration.*

■ *This loaf is large, so don't be scared to bake it well. An under-baked loaf will collapse after baking.*

■ *The egg wash gives extra shine and a golden-brown colour.*

Left: Assembling the grapes.

Above right: Arranging the grapes and vines.

Right: Cutting the ring around the edge of the loaf.

Chinese Barbecue Pork Buns

These typical Chinese buns are becoming very popular throughout Asia and are sold as a snack food alongside hot dogs and hamburgers. There's no end of options for fillings, so feel free to experiment. The buns are best eaten warm and are often re-steamed just prior to serving.

Dough

400g bread flour
5g fresh yeast (½ teaspoon active dry yeast)
210ml cool water
½ teaspoon salt
½ teaspoon baking powder

■ Place the flour, yeast and water in a bowl. Using a wooden spoon, combine the ingredients until a dough has formed. Tip the dough out onto a lightly floured bench and knead for 2–3 minutes. Lightly oil a bowl large enough to allow the dough to double in size. Put the dough in the bowl and cover it with plastic wrap. Leave in a warm place for 30 minutes.

Add 1 extra teaspoon of water, the salt and baking powder and incorporate them in the dough. Tip the dough out onto the bench. Knead for 15 minutes (resting every 3–4 minutes for 30 seconds) until the dough is smooth and elastic in consistency. The dough should be firm, so don't be tempted to add more water.

Return the dough to the bowl, cover it with plastic wrap and leave for 30 minutes, during which time you can make the Barbecue Pork Filling.

Barbecue Pork Filling

150g lean barbecue pork slices, pre-cooked
1 tablespoon soy sauce
1 tablespoon water
1 tablespoon oyster sauce
½ tablespoon sugar
½ tablespoon cornflour
½ tablespoon olive oil
½ small onion, finely chopped
½ teaspoon freshly grated ginger
freshly ground black pepper

■ Dice the pork finely and set aside. Place the soy sauce, water, oyster sauce, sugar and cornflour in a bowl and whisk them to a slurry. Set aside.

Heat the oil in a heavy-based frying pan or wok. Add the onion and cook until soft. Add the ginger and pork, cooking for 1–2 minutes. Drain any excess oil onto a paper towel. Add the sauce mixture, cooking over a gentle heat for 2–3 minutes until thickened. Season with pepper and set aside to cool.

Assembly and Baking

■ The dough should have almost doubled in size and started bubbling with gas.

Tip the dough out onto the floured bench. Mould it very gently and loosely into a sausage shape and cut into 10 equal portions. Mould each one into a small ball and place it on the bench. Cover the dough again with plastic wrap and leave for 15 minutes.

Roll each ball out to a circle 8.5cm in diameter. Place approximately 1 tablespoon of the Barbecue Pork Filling in the centre of each circle. Gather the dough up around the filling by pleating it along the edges. Bring the pleats up, twisting them securely and firmly. Place each dough ball on a 5cm x 5cm square of baking paper with the seam facing down. Cover the filled dough loosely with plastic wrap and leave in a warm place for 45–60 minutes or until almost double in size.

Bring a wok or saucepan of water to the boil with a bamboo steamer sitting on top, ensuring that there is space between the saucepan and steamer for the steam to escape. Place three or four buns in the steamer, allowing at least 3–4cm space between each bun for expansion during cooking. Put the steamer lid on and steam the buns for 20 minutes.

Remove the cooked buns. Repeat the steaming process with the remaining buns until they are all cooked. The larger the steamer, the more buns can be cooked at one time.

■ Makes 10 x 75g buns

Keys to Success

■ Pre-cooked barbecue pork slices are available from Asian food stores, as are bamboo steamers.

■ Feel free to substitute any of your favourite sweet or savoury fillings for the pork. Enjoy the versatility of this bun recipe.

■ Don't be overly generous with the fillings, or they will spill out during steaming and cause the buns to cook unevenly.

■ Keep the water level in the pan full and on a constant boil when steaming, to ensure quick and even cooking.

Sweet Red-Bean Kugelhopf

Here's a loaf that's based on a traditional European kugelhopf: a cross between bread and cake that is delightfully crisp on the outside and light in the centre. For an Asian twist, this recipe introduces the very popular Japanese red-bean paste as the filling. The result is an exotic East-meets-West treat to serve with coffee. Fresh is best!

Sweet Red-Bean Paste

110g dried red kidney beans
½ cup sugar
40g vegetable oil

■ The day before baking, wash the beans and place them in a small saucepan. Cover them with water and soak for approximately 10 hours, preferably overnight.

The next day, drain the beans, then cover with fresh water. Bring the beans and water to the boil. Simmer for 1½–2 hours, until the beans have softened. Remove them from the heat and drain. Process them in a liquidiser or blender until smooth. Add the sugar and blend again.

Heat the oil in a frying pan, add the beans and fry on a low to moderate heat for at least 5–7 minutes, pressing with a spatula to form a paste. Remove from the heat when the paste begins to dry. Set aside to cool.

Ferment

75g bread flour
25g fresh yeast (8g active dry yeast)
¼ teaspoon sugar
150ml milk, warmed to 30°C

■ Place the flour, yeast and sugar in a bowl and stir to combine. Pour in the milk. Stir the ingredients until a smooth batter results. Cover and leave the mixture in a warm place to ferment for 20 minutes until it becomes a frothy, spongy batter.

Final Dough

110g butter, softened
70g sugar
*50g egg (approximately 1 egg, broken
    then weighed)*
40g egg yolks (approximately 2)
300g bread flour
5g salt
1 quantity Ferment

■ Cream the butter and sugar until light and fluffy. Slowly add all the egg, beating between each addition. Beat until light and fluffy.

Mix all the ingredients to form a dough. Turn out onto a lightly floured bench and knead for 10–15 minutes. The dough will become smooth, elastic and a little sticky.

Lightly oil a bowl large enough to allow the dough to double in size. Place the dough in the bowl and cover it with plastic wrap. Leave in a warm place for 1 hour. Gently fold the dough onto itself in the bowl. Cover it again and leave for a further 30 minutes.

Assembly and Baking

melted butter, for greasing
icing sugar, for dusting

■ Tip the dough onto the floured bench. Roll it out to a rectangle 5mm thick. (Leave it for a few minutes when the rolling becomes difficult.) Spread the bean paste on the dough. Starting from a long edge, roll the dough to form a Swiss-roll shape. The final length depends on the mould size.

Join the ends to form a ring. Lightly grease a kugelhopf mould with melted butter. Place the dough in the mould smooth-side down.

Cover the kugelhopf with plastic wrap and leave in a warm place for approximately 1½ hours. Meanwhile, preheat the oven to 180–190°C. Bake the kugelhopf for approximately 30 minutes. Cool it on a rack. Dust with icing sugar.

■ Makes 1 x 1.1kg kugelhopf

Keys to Success

■   Avoid over-cooking the bean paste; this will make it too stiff.

■   Avoid the temptation to add more flour when kneading.

■   Kugelhopf or chimney moulds are available from kitchenware stores.

Gluten-Free Poppy-Seed Bread

Christchurch baker Marcus Braun created this 'no knead' recipe. It's dairy-free as well as wheat- and gluten-free, and it boasts both a moist interior and the crusty exterior of a wheat-based loaf. Dean has suggested some variations, but the possible additions and combinations are infinite.

460g rice flour
1½ tablespoons guar or xanthan gum
20g sugar or soft brown sugar
1½ teaspoons salt
40g finely ground polenta
25g poppy seeds
20g fresh yeast (5g active dry yeast)
350ml soy milk
100ml water, warmed to 25°C
30g vegetable oil
150g eggs (approximately 3 eggs, broken
    then weighed)
5ml cider vinegar
½ tablespoon each sesame and poppy seeds,
    for the topping
3–4 ice cubes

■ Place a small dish on the bottom shelf of the oven and preheat the oven to 220°C.

Place the dry ingredients and yeast in a bowl. Stir with a wooden spoon to combine evenly, making a small well in the middle. Place the soy milk, water, oil, eggs and vinegar in a separate bowl. Stir with a wooden spoon to combine evenly. Pour the wet ingredients into the well of the dry ingredients and mix gently. The resulting dough should be firm with a slightly elastic consistency.

Pour the dough into a greased loaf tin or tins. Cover with plastic wrap and leave in a warm place for 1 hour or until the dough has risen to approximately 1½cm from the top of the tin or tins. Remove the plastic wrap and sprinkle the seeds on the dough.

Place the loaf tin or tins in the oven, toss the ice cubes into the heated dish and quickly close the oven door. Bake for 20–25 minutes, or until the base of each loaf sounds hollow when tapped. Remove from the oven and cool on a rack.

Variations

■ Spicy Fruit and Nut Loaf — substitute 1 tablespoon of mixed spice for the 25g of poppy seeds. Add 150g of plump sultanas and 200g of walnuts (chopped and lightly roasted) to the dry ingredients. Sprinkle the top with sesame seeds before baking.

■ Italian Style Loaf — substitute 2 teaspoons of dried mixed herbs or oregano for the 25g of poppy seeds. When you add the wet ingredients to the dry ingredients, add 100g each of sundried tomatoes and black olives (both chopped) at the same time. Brush the top of the bread with olive oil as soon as you take it out of the oven.

■ Cheese and Bacon Loaf — when you add the wet ingredients to the dry ingredients, add 75g of onion (diced), 100g of bacon (cooked and diced) and 75g of cheese (grated) at the same time. Sprinkle grated cheese over the dough before baking.

■ Makes 1 x 1.2kg loaf or 2 smaller loaves

Keys to Success

■ Use 360g white rice flour and 100g brown rice flour if you wish.

■ This recipe will not work without either guar gum or xanthan gum. These are plant-derived alternatives to gluten. They come in powder form, are completely natural and can be purchased in small amounts from specialty health-food shops.

■ Feel free to substitute any other seeds of your choice for the poppy seeds.

Petite Pumpkin and Chive Baguettes

These petite baguettes are based on a traditional French recipe, which involves leaving the dough overnight to ferment. The great taste of pumpkin and chives makes these loaves ideal for serving with simple winter soups. Otherwise, serve filled with a soft white cheese or salty feta.

Pumpkin Purée with Chives

300g pumpkin, skin and seeds removed
¼ cup fresh chives, finely chopped

■ Make this the day before you plan to bake the baguettes. Preheat the oven to 220°C. Cut the pumpkin into small pieces, place on a baking tray and bake until soft, approximately 20 minutes. Alternatively cook in a microwave until soft. Mash, stir in the chives and set aside to cool before use in the Dough recipe below.

Dough

500g bread flour
10g salt
15g fresh yeast (5g active dry yeast)
1 quantity Pumpkin Purée with Chives
225ml water (or as needed)
3–4 ice cubes

■ The day before baking, place all the ingredients except the ice cubes in a bowl. Using a wooden spoon, combine until a dough has formed. Tip the dough out onto a lightly floured bench and knead for 10–15 minutes (resting every 3–4 minutes for 30 seconds) until the dough is smooth and elastic in consistency.

Lightly oil a bowl large enough to allow the dough to double in size. Put the dough in the bowl and cover it with plastic wrap. Leave in a warm place for 45 minutes until the dough is almost twice its original size. Tip the dough onto the bench and knock it back by gently folding it back onto itself three or four times.

Return the dough to the bowl and cover it again with plastic wrap. Leave it in a warm place for a further 30 minutes. Knock back the dough again, cover it with plastic wrap and refrigerate for approximately 10 hours, preferably overnight.

The next day, gently tip the dough onto a lightly floured bench and divide it into six equal portions. Shape each piece of dough into a small rectangle and roll up into a tight Swiss roll. Roll the dough out to small baguette shapes, 25–30cm long with tapered ends.

Place the unbaked baguettes on two baking trays lined with baking paper. Cover them with plastic wrap and allow to prove for 1–2 hours. Meanwhile, place a small dish on the bottom shelf of the oven and preheat the oven to 240°C.

Lightly dust the dough pieces with flour. Use a sharp knife to make four shallow diagonal slashes across the top of each baguette. Place the baking trays in the oven, toss the ice cubes into the heated dish and quickly close the oven door.

Bake for 15 minutes. Turn the trays around, reduce the oven temperature to 200°C and bake the loaves for a further 10 minutes, or until they are dark golden-brown and the bases sound hollow when tapped.

■ Makes 6 x 175g baguettes or 8 smaller loaves

Keys to Success

■ *The quantity of water needed for the dough depends on how moist the purée is. It may be necessary to add more flour to achieve a smooth, non-sticky dough.*

■ *Mould the baguettes tightly when giving them their final shape and length. During baking, this will help the cuts to burst open, enhancing the look of the loaves.*

■ *Dusting the dough lightly with flour before baking will achieve a rustic look.*

■ *The ice cubes will create plenty of steam in the oven. This helps the baguettes to rise.*

Vegetable and Cheese Barbecue Twist

Packed with fresh vegetables, garlic and cheese, this curvaceous loaf is excellent for summer picnics and barbecues. The vegetables make it moist, the combinations of flavours and textures are superb, and if warmed before serving, it's to die for! Try it sliced, drizzled with olive oil and quickly grilled on the barbecue.

300g bread flour
5g salt
1 teaspoon dried mixed herbs
5g fresh yeast (½ teaspoon active dry yeast)
5g olive oil
180ml warm water
20g red capsicum, finely diced
20g green capsicum, finely diced
20g onion, finely sliced
20g whole sweetcorn kernels, tinned or frozen
30g carrot, grated
20g Parmesan cheese, grated
1 tablespoon freshly crushed garlic
70g cheddar cheese, grated
3–4 ice cubes
olive oil, for glazing

■ Place the flour, salt, herbs, yeast, oil and water in a bowl. Using a wooden spoon, combine the ingredients until a dough has formed. Tip the dough out onto a lightly floured bench and knead for 10–15 minutes (resting every 3–4 minutes for 30 seconds). Add the vegetables and Parmesan and knead until they are fully incorporated. By the time you finish kneading, the dough should no longer be sticky; its consistency should be smooth and elastic.

Lightly oil a bowl large enough to allow the dough to double in size. Put the dough in the bowl and cover it with plastic wrap. Leave in a warm place for 45 minutes. Knock back the dough in the bowl by gently folding it back onto itself. Cover it again with plastic wrap and leave for a further 45 minutes.

Tip the dough out onto a floured bench and roll it out to a 25cm x 25cm square. Spread the garlic on the square and sprinkle the grated cheddar cheese over the top. Pat the garlic and cheese down lightly with the palm of your hand.

Brush water in a narrow strip along the bottom edge of the dough. Starting at the top, roll the dough up tightly to form a Swiss roll or pinwheel, approximately 30cm long. Using a large, sharp knife or dough scraper, make a single lengthways cut down the middle of the roll, all the way through the dough.

With the cut side of each dough strand facing up, twist the two strands around each other. Place the resulting plait on a baking

tray lined with baking paper and press the ends together firmly. Cover the dough with plastic wrap and allow to rise for 45–60 minutes. Meanwhile, place a small dish on the bottom shelf of the oven and preheat the oven to 220°C.

Place the baking tray in the oven, toss the ice cubes into the heated dish and quickly close the oven door. Bake for 20–25 minutes until light golden. Remove the loaf from the oven and brush immediately with olive oil.

■ Makes 1 x 700g loaf

Keys to Success

■ *If the vegetables are wet, lay them on a paper towel to absorb excess moisture before use.*

■ *During kneading, the dough will feel firm. Don't be tempted to add more water, as it will soften when the vegetables are added. If the dough is too soft and sticky after the vegetables are kneaded into it, add a small amount of flour.*

■ *If you cut the dough exactly down the middle, the twist will rise evenly during baking.*

■ *By pressing the plait ends together firmly, you will ensure that they do not unwind during baking.*

■ *Take care not to under-bake the bread, as this will cause it to collapse during cooling.*

■ *After the first 15 minutes' baking, you may need to turn the tray around and place baking paper over the twist to prevent burning.*

■ *To reheat the bread for serving warm with your barbecue, return it to a 200°C oven for 5 minutes.*

Beer and Walnut Butterflake Rolls

Dean was inspired to bake these rolls while in Germany, teaching Korean bakers about German rye-bread. The walnuts and caraway seeds complement the fermented, malty beer flavour. The technique for the dough layers has been a hit with many New Zealand restaurants, where Dean has made the rolls for serving with dinner.

400g bread flour
100g wholemeal flour
15g fresh yeast (5g active dry yeast)
10g salt
10g malt extract or treacle
10g honey
10g olive oil
2 teaspoons caraway seeds, lightly bruised
300ml Guinness
150g walnuts, chopped into small pieces
50g butter, melted
sesame seeds, for decoration
3–4 ice cubes

■ Place all the ingredients except the walnuts, butter, sesame seeds and ice cubes in a bowl. Using a wooden spoon, combine them until a dough has formed.

Tip the dough out onto a lightly floured bench. Knead for 10–15 minutes (resting every 3–4 minutes for 30 seconds); check frequently for stickiness. Add a little flour if necessary to make the dough less sticky, but be aware that this will happen with kneading. Add water if necessary to make the dough soft rather than firm. Add the walnuts and knead until well incorporated. The dough's consistency should be smooth and elastic.

Lightly oil a bowl large enough for the dough to double in size. Place the dough in the bowl and cover it with plastic wrap. Leave in a warm place until the dough has expanded to twice its original size, approximately 1½ hours.

Knock back the dough in the bowl by gently folding it back onto itself several times. Cover it again with plastic wrap and leave for a further 30 minutes.

Tip the dough out onto a lightly floured bench and roll it out to a rectangle of 20cm x 45cm x 1cm thick. Brush the entire top surface of the dough with melted butter. Fold the two ends into the centre and lightly press down. Brush the surface with melted butter and fold over again to create a book fold (four layers of dough with thin layers of butter separating them). Gently roll the dough out to 3–4cm thick.

Using a dough scraper, mark the dough surface into small squares, each approximately 5cm x 5cm. Cut the dough squares all the way through to achieve individual square rolls. Place each roll in greased standard muffin pans with the visible layers facing up. Sprinkle with sesame seeds. Cover with plastic wrap and prove for approximately 1 hour or until the dough pieces have almost doubled in size. Meanwhile, place a small dish on the bottom shelf of the oven and preheat the oven to 210ºC.

Place the pans in the oven, toss the ice cubes into the heated dish and quickly close the oven door. Bake for 15–20 minutes. Remove the rolls from the oven and brush immediately with melted butter. Remove from the pans and cool on a rack.

■ Makes 12 x 85g rolls

Keys to Success

■ *Dean prefers Guinness but a locally produced dark malt beer can be substituted. The malt flavour is essential. For a more subtle beer flavour, use 150ml beer and 150ml water.*

■ *Do not over-prove these little rolls or they will pop right out of the muffin pans.*

■ *The baked rolls are nutty brown and crisp on the outside with a flaky, buttery consistency inside.*

■ *The folding for these rolls is similar to that used for single turns in puff pastry (outlined in the Pastries, Pies and Tarts chapter).*

The ends of the rolled-out dough are folded into the middle.

More melted butter is applied to the dough, which is folded again to create four layers.

The cut rolls; rolls are placed into the muffin pans ready for their final rising.

Boston Buns

These are iconic Kiwi buns — otherwise known as traditional English Sally Lunns! The Boston is Dean's all-time favourite TV snack or afternoon-tea indulgence. Commercial versions use artificial raspberry flavours and colours in the icing, but Dean's icing uses only fresh butter, raspberries and icing sugar.

Dough

300g bread flour
5g salt
25g butter, softened
25g sugar
zest of 1 orange
15g fresh yeast (5g active dry yeast)
50g egg (approximately 1 egg, broken
  then weighed)
150ml water, warmed to 25°C
75g plump currants, washed the previous day
75g plump sultanas, washed the previous day
100ml water, for glazing
30g sugar, for glazing

■ Place all the ingredients except the currants, sultanas and glaze components into a bowl. Using a wooden spoon, combine the ingredients until a dough has formed. Tip the dough out onto a lightly floured bench and knead for 15–20 minutes (resting every 3–4 minutes for 30 seconds) until it is smooth and elastic in consistency. Add the currants and sultanas and continue to knead the dough very gently until they are incorporated.

Lightly oil a bowl large enough to allow the dough to double in size. Place the dough in the bowl and cover it with plastic wrap. Leave in a warm place for 45 minutes. Knock back the dough in the bowl by gently folding it back onto itself. Cover it again with plastic wrap and leave for a further 30 minutes.

Tip the dough out onto the bench, divide it into two equal portions and mould into balls. Allow these to rest on the bench for 5–10 minutes, then press them out to a circle 15cm in diameter using the palm of your hand. Place the two flat buns at least 5cm apart on a baking tray lined with baking paper. Cover them with plastic wrap and leave to rise for 45–60 minutes. Preheat the oven to 180–190°C at this point.

Bake the buns for approximately 15 minutes or until golden-brown. Meanwhile, prepare a sugar glaze, to be brushed onto the buns immediately after baking: place 100ml water and 30g sugar in a small saucepan and heat until boiling (alternatively, heat in the microwave until boiling). Remove from the heat.

Remove the buns from the oven and brush with the sugar glaze. Allow the buns and glaze to cool completely before applying the icing.

To Finish

100g unsalted butter, softened
100g icing sugar
50g raspberries (if frozen, thaw at room
  temperature first)
20g coconut threads

■ Beat the butter and sugar until light, creamy and fluffy, preferably using an electric mixer with a beater attachment. Add the raspberries and beat until they are evenly distributed.

Using a palette knife or the back of a spoon, spread the raspberry icing on top of the buns in a circular pattern. Immediately sprinkle coconut over the icing.

Enjoy buttered slices of Boston Bun with your favourite tea.

■ Makes 2 x 300g buns

Keys to Success

■ *Wash the dried fruits in hot water the day before baking, then leave them overnight in a covered container to make them delectably plump. Knead them into the dough very gently to prevent them from breaking up.*

■ *The high sugar, butter and egg content in this recipe make the dough very soft; it will also be a little sticky. Don't be tempted to add extra flour. The stickiness will disappear during the kneading and rising stages.*

Dean's Pain au Levain

You can't go past this loaf's tangy taste and aroma. The recipe combines great natural ingredients — including the unique starter you've nurtured— and techniques Dean has perfected over the years. He cuts his signature 'B' for baker into his levain loaves. When you've created your own pain au levain, you've earned the right to make your mark!

300g bread flour
50g wholemeal flour
130g Levain Starter (see page 52)
½ teaspoon malt flour or liquid malt extract
⅛ teaspoon fresh yeast (very small pinch active
*   dry yeast)*
1¼ teaspoons salt
250ml chilled water
3–4 ice cubes

■ The day before you plan to bake, place all the ingredients except the ice cubes in a bowl. Using a wooden spoon, combine the ingredients until a dough has formed. Tip the dough out onto a lightly floured bench and knead for 15–20 minutes (resting every 3–4 minutes for 30 seconds) until the dough is soft, smooth and elastic in consistency.

Lightly oil a bowl large enough to allow the dough to double in size. Place the dough in the bowl and cover it with plastic wrap. Leave in a warm place for approximately 3 hours, until the dough is almost twice its original size. Tip the dough onto the bench and knock it back, gently folding it back onto itself three or four times. Return the dough to the bowl and cover again with plastic wrap. Leave for 1 hour in a warm place. The dough should be very bubbly by the end of this time.

Very gently, tip the dough onto the bench and mould it into a ball. Cover it with plastic wrap and leave for 15–20 minutes. Meanwhile, lay a tea-towel inside a round small to medium-sized cane basket or bowl and coat it evenly with flour.

Mould the dough into its final ball shape, making sure it is firm and tight. Gently place the dough into the prepared bowl with the scrunched-up seam side facing up and the smooth side down. Cover it with plastic wrap and leave in a warm place for approximately 45 minutes, then refrigerate for approximately 10 hours, preferably overnight.

The next day, 2–2½ hours before you plan to bake, remove the dough from the refrigerator and leave it at room temperature, with the plastic wrap intact. Meanwhile, place a heavy baking tray or a baking stone in the oven and a small dish on the bottom shelf. Preheat the oven to 250°C.

Remove the preheated baking tray and very gently tip your dough onto it. Using a sharp knife or razor blade, cut a symbol or letter of your choice into the top of the loaf. Place the baking tray on a lower to middle shelf of the oven, toss the ice cubes into the heated dish and quickly close the oven door.

Bake for 20 minutes. Turn the tray around, reduce the temperature to 200°C and bake for a further 10–15 minutes or until the loaf is dark golden-brown and the base sounds hollow when tapped. Remove the bread from the oven and cool on a rack.

■ Makes 1 x 735g loaf

Keys to Success

■ *The tiny amount of commercial yeast in the dough is there merely as a back-up for the levain starter.*

■ *Malt flour can be purchased from specialty shops.*

■ *Refrigerating the moulded dough overnight will further develop the loaf's flavour and texture.*

■ *Use the indentation test to check when your dough is ready to go into the oven. Press the side of the dough lightly with a fingertip. If it quickly resumes its original shape, more rising time is required. If the indentation lessens but the mark remains, the dough is ready to be baked.*

■ *Bake your loaf on a heated baking stone or baking tray. If you use a baking stone, place this in the oven an hour before baking. A baking stone is ideal as it conducts heat well, dispersing it evenly.*

Caramelised Garlic and Tomato Focaccia

A versatile treat: perfect eaten in large wedges as a picnic food, or served on a wintry night to accompany a stew or hearty soup. The Caramelised Garlic Topping certainly adds flavour to this flat bread, which was developed by Dean's London-based friend Dan Lepard, an award-winning baking author.

Dough

275g bread flour
25g wholemeal flour
100g Levain Starter (see page 52)
5g salt
15g olive oil
5g fresh yeast (½ teaspoon active dry yeast)
170ml warm water

■ Place all the ingredients in a bowl. Combine them until a dough has formed. Tip the dough out onto a lightly floured bench and knead for 15–20 minutes (resting every 3–4 minutes for 30 seconds) until the dough is smooth and elastic in consistency.

Lightly oil a bowl large enough to allow the dough to double in size. Put the dough in the bowl and cover it with plastic wrap. Leave in a warm place for approximately 1½ hours. By the end of this time it should have started to bubble with gas.

Tip the dough out onto the bench. Mould it very gently and loosely into a ball. Cover it again with plastic wrap and leave for 15 minutes. Meanwhile, make the topping as below.

Caramelised Garlic Topping

2 heads garlic, separated into cloves
2 tablespoons olive oil
2 tablespoons water
1 tablespoon balsamic vinegar
3 tablespoons sugar
½ teaspoon salt
¼ teaspoon freshly ground black pepper
1 sprig fresh rosemary, chopped

■ Bring a saucepan of water to the boil. Blanch the garlic for 2 minutes. Refresh it in cold water, peel and set aside.

Place the oil in a heavy-based frying pan over a moderate heat. When the oil starts to shimmer, add the garlic and sauté for 1 minute, taking care not to burn. Add the water and vinegar. As the mixture bubbles, add the sugar, salt, pepper and rosemary.

Reduce the heat to its lowest setting and simmer the mixture for 3–4 minutes until a syrup is formed and the garlic is soft. Transfer to a bowl, cool until needed, then use as below.

Assembly and Baking

3½ tablespoons olive oil
leaves of 1 sprig fresh rosemary
5 firm cherry tomatoes, halved
1½ tablespoons water

■ Using the palm of your hand, flatten the dough to a circle 25cm in diameter. Line a baking tray with baking paper, drizzle 2 tablespoons of the olive oil in the centre and smear the oil in a circle 25cm in diameter. Place the dough on the circle. Use your fingertips to press the dough repeatedly, right across the top.

Stud the dough surface evenly with the garlic cloves (discard the syrup), rosemary and tomatoes. Drizzle the water and the remaining olive oil over the top.

Cover the dough loosely with plastic wrap and leave in a warm place for approximately 1 hour. Meanwhile, preheat the oven to 230–240°C.

Place the baking tray and dough in the oven and bake for 12–15 minutes. Remove the focaccia from the oven, brush with olive oil immediately and cool on a rack.

■ Makes 1 x 650g focaccia

Keys to Success

■ The water and olive oil create a pleasing contrast,
with pale white and golden-brown colours on the
crust. The heat colours other parts of the crust an
attractive russet.

■ This focaccia can be made without the Levain Starter,
although it will lose some flavour. Increase the fresh yeast
quantity to 10g (1 teaspoon of active dry yeast) and the
water quantity to 220ml.

■ When shaping the dough into a circle, leave it to
rest for a few minutes from time to time.

Chocolate, Pecan and Cranberry Sourdough

One of Dean's favourite bread recipes. Why not toast it and treat it like a bagel?
It's superb spread with cream cheese and a little top-quality strawberry preserve.

350g bread flour
200g Levain Starter (see page 52)
20g cocoa powder
230ml water, warmed to 25°C
1¼ teaspoons salt
80g dried cranberries
80g pecans, chopped
80g chocolate pieces, broken (or chocolate chips)
3–4 ice cubes

■ Place the flour, starter, cocoa and water in a bowl. Using a wooden spoon, combine the ingredients until a dough has formed. Tip the dough out onto a lightly floured bench and knead for 10–15 minutes (resting every 3–4 minutes for 30 seconds) until the dough is smooth and elastic in consistency.

Lightly oil a bowl large enough to allow the dough to double in size. Place the dough in the bowl and cover it with plastic wrap. Leave in a warm place for 20 minutes .

Tip the dough out onto the bench again, add the salt and knead for a further 3–4 minutes, until the salt is fully incorporated and the dough is smooth and elastic in consistency. Add the cranberries, pecans and chocolate pieces. Knead until they are incorporated and evenly distributed throughout the dough.

Return the dough to the bowl and cover it with plastic wrap. Leave in a warm place until the dough has expanded to almost twice its original size, approximately 3 hours.

Tip the dough onto the bench and knock it back by gently folding it back onto itself three or four times. Return the dough to the bowl and cover it again with plastic wrap. Leave in a warm place for 1 hour. Meanwhile, lay a tea-towel inside a round cane basket or medium-sized round bowl and dust it lightly with flour.

Tip the dough out onto the bench. Gently mould it into a ball by cupping your hands around it and moving them in a circular motion, easing and stretching the surface of the dough. Be very gentle or the surface will rip and the appearance of the finished loaf will be spoilt. The final shape will be mostly smooth and round except for the base, which will be rough and scrunched up.

Place the loaf into the prepared basket or bowl, seam side up, and cover it with plastic wrap. Leave to rise for 2–2½ hours or until almost doubled in size. Meanwhile, place a baking stone or heavy baking tray in the oven and a small dish on the bottom shelf of the oven. Preheat the oven to 240–250°C.

Lightly dust a small, cold baking tray with semolina or flour and gently tip the dough onto it. Using a razor blade or sharp knife, make eight cuts (each up to ½cm deep) in the top of the loaf.

Immediately, and very gently, transfer the dough from the cold tray to the heated tray or stone in the oven. Toss the ice cubes into the heated dish and quickly close the oven door.

Bake for 20 minutes, then turn the heat down to 200°C and check the loaf for even baking. Turn the tray around if necessary. Bake for a further 15–20 minutes. Remove from the oven. Cool on a rack.

■ Makes 1 x 1.050kg loaf

Keys to Success

■ Refrigerate the chocolate pieces the night before baking: this will prevent them from melting when being kneaded into the dough.

■ The salt is added much later than the other dry ingredients; otherwise it (together with the cocoa) will slow down the action of the wild yeast.

■ For best results, bake on a baking stone, preheated for an hour. Baking stones conduct heat well, dispersing it evenly.

■ Don't expect this loaf to be light and fluffy in texture. The high proportions of fruit, nuts and chocolate will make it dense and compact.

Sage, Chilli and Onion Tortillas

Create your own wraps using these freshly made tortillas: just fill and roll! A Mexican-style combo might include spicy meats, lettuce, salsa, grated cheese and a touch of chilli sauce — but really, the possibilities are endless.

300g standard flour
5g salt
30g olive oil
5g baking powder
15g onion, finely chopped
1 tablespoon fresh chopped or 1 teaspoon
  dried sage
1 tablespoon finely chopped chilli, seeds removed
175ml water, warmed to 25°C

■ Place all the ingredients in a bowl. Mix them until a firm dough has formed. Tip the dough out onto a lightly floured bench and knead for approximately 10 minutes (resting every 3–4 minutes for 30 seconds) until the dough is smooth and elastic in consistency.

Place a baking tray on the middle shelf of the oven and preheat the oven to 250ºC.

Using a sharp knife or dough scraper, cut the dough into 10 equal portions. Mould each into a ball, place on the bench and cover with plastic wrap. Leave the dough pieces to rest for 20 minutes.

Roll each dough ball out on the bench to form a circle 18cm in diameter and 2–3mm thick.

Place two tortillas on a cold baking tray lined with baking paper. Slide the tortillas and paper onto the preheated baking tray and bake for 1–2 minutes, then flip them over and bake for 1 minute. Remove from the oven and repeat with the remaining unbaked tortillas.

As the tortillas are baked, stack them on top of each other and cover well with a cloth.

■ Makes 10 x 50g tortillas

Keys to Success

■ *Remember this recipe has no yeast, so don't expect it to puff up and rise!*

■ *Ensure the bench is well floured before you roll the dough pieces out on it; otherwise they will stick and tear. Brush off excess flour before baking.*

■ *An alternative to baking tortillas in the oven is to cook them on a very hot griddle or large heavy-based frying pan. Turn them halfway through cooking.*

■ *If you wish to use a baking stone instead of a baking tray, place this in the oven an hour before baking. A baking stone is ideal as it conducts heat well, dispersing it evenly.*

■ *Tortillas are meant to be soft (not crisp) and quite pale. Avoid over-baking, as this will dry them out and they will break when filled and rolled up.*

■ *Stacking and covering the baked tortillas will keep them soft and prevent them from drying out. Use as required but note they are best eaten the day of baking, preferably within an hour or two after you've taken them out of the oven.*

Korean Corn Bread

While travelling and working in Seoul, South Korea, Dean frequently encounters this wonderful bread in high-class bakeries and pâtisseries. Chang-Hyun Ahn kindly shared his recipe, to which Dean has added whole sweetcorn kernels. Thanks to its subtle sweetcorn flavour, it's a treat just sliced and spread thinly with butter.

160g bread flour
120g finely ground polenta
15g baking powder
5g salt
60g sugar
60g butter, softened
100ml milk
2 small eggs, beaten
50g canned whole sweetcorn kernels, drained
   and dried
25g chilled butter, cut into 5mm cubes
1 egg, for egg wash
2 tablespoons water, for egg wash

■ Sift all the dry ingredients into a bowl. Add the softened butter, milk and 2 eggs. Using a wooden spoon, combine until a dough has formed.

Tip the dough onto a lightly floured bench and knead for approximately 5 minutes. Add the sweetcorn and gently mix it in. Mould the dough into a rough ball shape and cover it with plastic wrap. Leave on the bench for 10–15 minutes.

Meanwhile, preheat the oven to 180°C. Make an egg wash by whisking the remaining egg and water together.

Using a scraper, divide the dough into three equal portions. Mould each into a stubby loaf with a fat middle and tapered ends. Place the loaves on a baking tray lined with baking paper.

Using a sharp serrated knife, cut lengthways down the middle of each dough piece, 1–1½ cm deep. Lightly brush each dough piece with the egg wash, ensuring an even coating. Place three cubes of butter inside each deep cut.

Bake for 20–25 minutes until the rolls are a rich golden colour. Remove from the oven and place on a cooling rack. Serve within one day of making or store immediately in an airtight container for use the next day.

■ Makes 3 x 220g loaves

Keys to Success

■ The polenta used in this recipe should be so finely ground that it is almost powder-like. If necessary, blend it in a food processor to achieve this texture.

■ The relatively small quantity of wheat flour means that the dough will be a little sticky to handle. During final shaping, ensure the bench is well floured to prevent the dough from sticking.

■ Be careful while baking: the loaves will darken quickly due to their sugar content.

Spinach, Chilli and Feta Damper

Bushmen who tended sheep in the Australian outback first baked damper in heavy pans over an open fire, probably in an attempt to recreate Irish soda bread. Various immigrant communities have contributed to Australian cuisine — especially the Greek population — so the spinach, chilli and sheep feta in this damper give it an appropriate twist.

500g bread flour
5g salt
40g baking powder
30g milk powder
freshly ground black pepper
65g butter, softened
350ml water, warmed to 25°C
120g sheep feta, roughly cut into small cubes
100g spinach, washed, dried and roughly chopped
3 medium-sized fresh red chillies, seeds removed,
    then finely chopped

■ Sift the flour, salt, baking powder and milk powder into a bowl. Add the pepper and butter. Using your fingertips, rub the butter into the dry ingredients until the mixture resembles breadcrumbs. Make a well large enough to contain the water, then slowly add the water. Gently combine the ingredients by hand, taking care not to over-mix.

When the dough is almost combined, with wet and floury patches remaining, add the feta, spinach and chilli. Fold them into the dough to achieve a roughly textured mass. Again, be careful not to over-mix.

Divide the dough into three equal portions. On a floured bench, mould the dough pieces very lightly into balls, with the smoothest part facing upwards. Place the dough pieces on a baking tray lined with baking paper. Preheat the oven to 220–230°C.

Using the palm of your hand, gently flatten each dough piece into a circle 15cm in diameter. Lightly dust with flour. Leave the unbaked dampers to rest in a cool place for 15 minutes.

Divide each damper into quarters, using a large knife or metal scraper, cutting only three-quarters of the way through.

Bake for 15 minutes. Remove from the oven and place on a cooling rack.

■ Makes 3 x 400g loaves

Keys to Success

■ The ingredients can be changed to suit your tastes. Try substituting 250g of partly cooked pumpkin cubes and 4 tablespoons of crunchy peanut-butter for the feta, spinach and chilli.

■ If no milk powder is available, use 175ml of fresh full-cream milk and 175ml of water (to replace 30g of milk powder and 350ml of water).

■ Damper dough is wet, sticky and scone-like. Avoid over-mixing as this will develop the flour proteins, thereby toughening the bread.

■ Avoid over-baking, as this will result in a dry damper. The baked consistency should be moist and scone-like.

■ Damper is what's known as a quick bread: quick to make, because it requires no rising time and little or no kneading. However, damper also becomes stale quickly, so eat it within hours of making it, when it's still deliciously fresh.

Hazelnut and Quark Breakfast Plaits

These sweet loaves have German origins and can be made in a short time, because they're baking-powder-risen. Moist and tender, they make a great start to the day and are perfect for a special brunch.

Filling

100g ground hazelnuts
50g ground almonds
1 large egg
¾ tablespoon standard flour
70g sugar
½ teaspoon pure vanilla essence
1 teaspoon rum

■ Lightly toast the ground hazelnuts and almonds in a dry frying-pan, tossing and stirring constantly to prevent them from burning. Remove the nuts from the heat when they turn light amber in colour. Leave them to cool.

Place all the ingredients (including the nuts) in a bowl. Beat them with a wooden spoon until a smooth and spreadable paste is formed. Set aside.

Dough

300g standard flour
80g caster sugar
1 tablespoon baking powder
150g quark
100ml milk, warmed to room temperature
50ml vegetable oil
1 teaspoon pure vanilla essence
¼ teaspoon salt
1 egg, for egg wash
2 tablespoons water, for egg wash

■ Sift the flour, sugar and baking powder into a bowl. Add the quark, milk, oil, vanilla and salt. Using a wooden spoon, combine the ingredients to form a dough.

Tip the dough out onto a lightly floured bench and knead intensively for 2 minutes. Cut the dough into two equal portions and shape these into squares. Roll each dough piece out on a floured bench to form larger squares, each measuring approximately 25cm x 25cm.

Whisk the egg and water together to make an egg wash. Spread half the filling evenly on a dough sheet, leaving a 1cm strip free at the bottom end. Egg-wash the strip. Starting at the top, tightly roll the dough sheet up to achieve a Swiss roll or pinwheel approximately 25cm long. Repeat the filling, egg-washing and rolling process with the other dough sheet.

Using a sharp knife or dough scraper, make a single lengthways cut down the middle of each roll, all the way through. You will now have four separate strands. At this point, preheat the oven to 170°C.

Take two strands and, with the cut side of each strand facing up, twist them around each other. Press the ends together firmly. Twist and press the other two strands.

Place the two resulting plaits on a baking tray lined with baking paper. Keep the plaits well apart so they don't join together during baking. Brush with egg wash and allow them to rest for 15–20 minutes on the bench before baking.

Bake for 25–30 minutes, turning the tray halfway through baking. Meanwhile, make the Apricot Glaze as below.

Apricot Glaze

4 tablespoons apricot jam
3 tablespoons water

■ Place the jam and water in a small saucepan and bring to the boil, stirring constantly. Strain the mixture through a sieve and brush onto the plaits while both the glaze and the loaves are hot.

■ Makes 2 x 400g loaves

Keys to Success

■   Quark is a type of soft cheese; if quark is not available, substitute sour cream.

■   This bread is ideal eaten still warm from baking. However, it's also great warmed in a microwave a day or so later.

■   Avoid over-mixing the dough, as this will make it too sticky.

■   When cutting the filled, rolled dough into strands, take care to cut exactly down the middle, so that the plaits will rise evenly during baking.

Chocolate, Rum and Raisin Bread Pudding

This is a wicked, boozy chocolate pudding: a real indulgence, particularly in the winter months. Serve warm with fresh cream.

100g raisins
4 tablespoons rum
1 standard baked baguette, sliced
   (approximately 30 slices)
butter, softened (as needed)
1 teaspoon cinnamon
100g chocolate, roughly chopped
3 eggs
2 tablespoons caster sugar
500ml milk
125ml cream
1 teaspoon pure vanilla essence
100g chocolate, roughly chopped, for melting
1 tablespoon caster sugar, for sprinkling
icing sugar, for dusting

■ On the day before baking, place the raisins in a bowl and sprinkle with rum. Cover them and leave to soak for approximately 6 hours, preferably overnight. Toss occasionally to ensure the raisins absorb all the rum.

The next day, butter each slice of bread (one side only). Place a layer of bread in a greased baking dish, butter side up. Sprinkle half the rum-soaked raisins, cinnamon and first quantity of chocolate on top. Layer again with bread and sprinkle with the remaining other ingredients as above. Place a final layer of bread on top.

Put the eggs and sugar in a large bowl and whisk together very briefly. Place the milk, cream and vanilla in a saucepan and heat them over a moderate heat until just boiling. Remove from the heat and add the second quantity of chocolate. Leave to stand for 5 minutes, then whisk until the chocolate has completely melted.

Whisk the chocolate mixture into the eggs and sugar to create a thin custard. Pour the custard over the bread slices. Press the slices down into the mixture to completely submerge them in the custard. Sprinkle with the second quantity of caster sugar. Cover the baking dish with baking paper and leave the pudding to soak for approximately 30 minutes. Meanwhile, preheat the oven to 160°C.

Bake the pudding for 20 minutes with the baking paper still covering it. Remove the paper and bake for a further 50–60 minutes. Remove the pudding from the oven when it has risen slightly, the custard has just set and the bread slices are crisp around the edges. Allow the pudding to cool slightly, dust it with icing sugar and serve warm with cream.

■ Makes 1 x 1-litre pudding

Keys to Success

■ *Day-old bread is better than fresh bread, as it will absorb the custard more readily.*

■ *Feel free to use spare smaller-sized baguettes from the recipe on page 51 – if you have any left over, which is most unlikely!*

■ *Soaking the raisins in rum for several hours is important – to make them plump and juicy. If you do not allow enough time for this, your pudding will have too much 'free' liquid sloshing around.*

■ *For a visual variation, make and bake this pudding in four to six individual portions – either in ramekins or teacups. Bake them at 160°C for 35-40 minutes in total.*

cakes
and
cookies

Making Cakes

Most cultures have traditions of cakes. Many of these are pleasurable, celebratory and even luxurious additions to the basic diet. The range of cakes is vast, from special-occasion and celebration cakes to the tiny cakes and cookies that simply sweeten the end of a meal or assuage the appetite between the main meals of the day.

How It Works

■ Air doesn't appear in the ingredient list but it is an essential ingredient in a successful cake. When you whisk the eggs and sugar and sift the flour, air enters the mix. If you over-mix, you will pound out those precious air bubbles.

Butter (or oil), if included in the recipe, will trap the air, resulting in a foamy consistency in the mixture and ultimately maximising the lightness and volume of the baked cake. Butter also plays a tenderising role: it coats the flour proteins, reducing their contact with moisture and preventing the gluten network from developing. It results in a soft, melt-in-the-mouth sensation when the cake is eaten and will enhance the cake's keeping qualities.

In the oven, the batter becomes quite fluid as the temperature rises. (If knocked at this stage, the cake could lose volume.) The trapped air begins to expand. If baking powder has been used, it releases carbon dioxide. This results in the air bubbles becoming larger and joining together. The volume of the batter increases and the proteins of the flour and egg stretch to accommodate the expanding gases.

The still-increasing heat results in steam, which — together with the butter — assists in aeration (rising). It also causes the starch of the flour to absorb moisture. The expanding proteins begin to coagulate (set). The sugar near the crust caramelises to give the golden-brown colour.

Baking and Cooling

PRODUCT	TEMPERATURE	TIME
Sponge Cakes	180–200°C	20–30 minutes
Swiss Rolls	220–230°C	5–7 minutes
Other Cakes	170–180°C	30–90 minutes depending on the batter consistency
Biscuits and Cookies	170–190°C	12–20 minutes depending on the size and dough consistency

Times and temperatures will vary from oven to oven.

Basic Sponge Cake

A basic sponge consists of sugar, eggs and flour. Sometimes melted butter is added to enhance softness and keeping qualities. Cocoa powder, instant coffee, pure vanilla essence and ground nuts of various kinds can also be added for different flavours and textures.

4 eggs, at room temperature
125g caster sugar
125g standard flour
50g butter, melted
few drops pure vanilla essence (optional)

■ Preheat the oven to 190°C.

Whisk the eggs and sugar together (preferably in an electric mixer, using the whisk attachment), until they are thick and foamy. Check for readiness by drizzling a little of the mixture onto the remainder. The drizzled mixture should stay on top for about 10 seconds before being absorbed.

Sift the flour and carefully fold it through the mixture until it is three-quarters incorporated. Add the butter and vanilla (or any other flavourings), and fold them through gently. Avoid over-mixing. Immediately place the mixture in a greased and floured cake tin.

Bake until the sponge is set, 25–30 minutes. Remove from the oven and set aside in the tin for 5–10 minutes.

If you plan to keep the sponge for use in the future, cool it, cover in plastic wrap and freeze until required.

■ Makes 1 x 20cm round sponge

Keys to Success

■ *Take care to measure accurately and to follow all instructions when baking sponges or other cakes and cookies. There is not much room for spontaneous innovation or alteration: like bread-making, this is a scientific process involving a formula and requiring precision.*

■ *Ensure that your equipment is clean and grease-free.*

■ *Avoid over-mixing when folding in the flour and butter, as this will reduce the volume of the baked sponge.*

■ *Bake the sponge as soon as you have combined the ingredients.*

■ *To test whether the sponge is baked, press it lightly with a fingertip. The surface should spring back, showing no sign of your touch.*

■ *Once cakes and cookies are out of the oven, you should leave them in the tin or on the baking tray for 5-10 minutes to settle and become firm. This will prevent damage to the structure.*

■ *If time is limited and you are new to cake-making, select two or three cake recipes to practise with and perfect. Everyone should have a small repertoire of cakes to bake for the enjoyment of friends and family.*

Chocolate Pistachio Madeleines

The madeleine entered culinary and literary history when Marcel Proust described it as 'a sea shell cake'. Here, pistachios and chocolate chips have been added to the classic batter. Finish your madeleines with melted chocolate and more pistachios. Best eaten the day of baking!

250g standard flour
1 teaspoon baking powder
pinch of salt
45g pistachios, coarsely chopped
75g chocolate chips
melted butter, for greasing
flour, for dusting
3 eggs
200g caster sugar
80ml milk, at room temperature
2–3 drops pure vanilla essence
125g butter, melted
100g dark chocolate, for decoration
2 tablespoons pistachios, coarsely chopped,
    for decoration

■ Preheat the oven to 210ºC. Sift the flour, baking powder and salt together. Toss the pistachios and chocolate chips through the dry mixture. Set aside. Lightly grease the madeleine moulds with melted butter and coat them in flour, tapping to remove any excess flour.

Whisk the eggs and sugar until the mixture is thick and creamy, preferably using an electric mixer with a whisk attachment. Gradually add the milk and vanilla, mixing on a low speed.

Fold the dry ingredients into the batter gently, until they are three-quarters mixed in. Fold in the 125g melted butter carefully, until you achieve a creamy, supple paste.

Using a tablespoon, three-quarters fill each mould (using approximately 25g of mixture for each). Bake for 9–10 minutes or until the madeleines spring back when lightly touched with your fingertip. The exact quantities of filling and the baking times depend on the size of the moulds.

Remove the madeleines from their moulds immediately and cool on a rack. Meanwhile, melt the chocolate in a bowl over hot water.

Dip the shell-patterned side of each madeleine in the melted chocolate. Sprinkle pistachios onto the chocolate before it sets.

■ Makes 24 madeleines

Keys to Success

■ Remove the butter from the heat when its melted consistency is smooth and creamy. This will give the baked madeleines a rich, buttery taste. Don't continue heating the butter until it separates into water and butter fat, as this will give the cakes a greasy taste and texture.

■ Warming the eggs and sugar will make it easier to whisk them into a thick, fluffy, creamy foam, which is essential for a light cake structure. Place the bowl over a saucepan of warm water from time to time during the whisking stage.

■ When you fold the dry ingredients into the batter, minimise mixing so you retain the air in what is essentially a sponge mixture.

■ If your madeleine moulds can hold only part of the mixture, bake in batches. Cool just-used moulds quickly before you bake the rest of the mixture.

■ These tiny cakes bake really fast. Avoid over-baking, as this will dry them out.

Moroccan Honey and Mint Syrup Cake

The Moroccan combination of mint and honey comes through well in this sweet, moist cake. Perfect with a dollop of natural yoghurt sweetened with honey and mint, and freshly made mint tea.

Batter

160g butter, softened
310g sugar
1½ teaspoons dried or fresh chopped mint
6 eggs
230g desiccated coconut
210g self-raising flour

■ Preheat the oven to 150ºC.
  Beat the butter, sugar and mint until they begin to change colour. Add small quantities of the egg, coconut and flour, beating well between each addition to prevent the mixture from curdling. Repeat until you have used these ingredients up.
  Line a lightly greased spring-release cake-tin with baking paper. Pour the batter in. Bake for 1–1½ hours (you can make the Mint Syrup during this time).
  Check the cake is baked by inserting a skewer in the centre. If it comes out clean, the cake is ready. Remove from the oven and allow it to cool in the tin for 5–10 minutes.

Mint Syrup

200ml water
180g sugar
1½ cups roughly chopped fresh mint

■ Place the water, sugar and mint in a saucepan. Bring to the boil, stirring occasionally to ensure the sugar is dissolved. Remove from the heat and allow to cool for 30–45 minutes. Strain through a sieve and discard the mint leaves. Use the syrup as directed.

Assembly

75g butter
180g honey
180g flaked almonds

■ Preheat the oven to 170ºC.
  With the cake still in the tin, prick 60–70 holes in the top. Pour the Mint Syrup evenly over the cake, allowing it to soak in.
  Place the butter, honey and almonds in a saucepan and melt together, stirring until well combined. Do not allow to boil. Remove from the heat and immediately spread this topping on the cake.
  Place the cake back in the oven and bake the topping to a light amber colour, approximately 15 minutes. Remove and allow to cool in the tin for 20–30 minutes. Remove the cake from the tin carefully and remove the baking paper gently while still warm.
  Dust with icing sugar before serving.

■ Makes 1 x 20cm round cake

Keys to Success

■ *Ensure your self-raising flour is as fresh as possible.*

■ *Don't cream the butter and sugar until they are light and fluffy, as this will result in an open and light-textured cake. This is a dense, hearty cake.*

■ *Prepare the Mint Syrup in advance and allow to cool before using. This will enhance the mint flavour.*

■ *Make the honey and almond topping just as you need it: it must be warm when you spread it on top of the cake.*

■ *When the cake is in the oven for the second time, avoid burning the topping.*

Spicy Armagnac Eccles Cakes

These are old favourites that were once served as part of a sumptuous English afternoon-tea spread. Soaking the filling in Armagnac introduces extra flavour that complements the spice. Please use only butter pastry, as this creates the special 'melt in the mouth' quality.

Butter Puff Pastry

■ Use one quantity of the Butter Puff Pastry on page 12. Make it a day ahead and store in the refrigerator, in plastic wrap.

Filling

200g currants
5 tablespoons Armagnac
25g butter, softened
70g soft brown sugar
80g cake crumbs
30g golden syrup
½ teaspoon mixed spice
zest of ½ lemon

■ Soak the currants in the Armagnac for at least 3–4 hours, preferably overnight. They will become plump and juicy.

The next day, use a wooden spoon to beat the butter and sugar together until soft and creamy, but not light and fluffy. Add the remaining ingredients, including the currants, and combine well. The filling should be soft but firm; you may need to adjust the consistency by adding a few more cake crumbs.

Assembly and Baking

water
caster sugar

■ On a lightly floured bench, gently roll the pastry out to approximately 4mm thick. Cut into 10cm x 10cm squares. Place one heaped tablespoon of the filling in the centre of each square. Using a pastry brush dipped in water, lightly brush the edges of the squares. Bring the corners of pastry into the centre of each square and pinch them together. Gather in the remaining pastry and seal it.

With the palm of your hand, flatten each filled pastry slightly. Turn it over so the newly sealed side is on the bench, then lightly roll it out to achieve a 7–8cm circle. Brush the top and sides with water. Dip each pastry into caster sugar, coating it evenly.

Line a baking tray with baking paper and place the cakes on the tray. Using a sharp knife, cut two vents into the top of each cake. Allow the pastry to rest for at least 60 minutes; meanwhile preheat the oven to 210–220ºC.

Bake the cakes for approximately 20 minutes or until the sugar has turned golden-brown and just started to caramelise. Remove from the oven and allow to cool.

■ Makes 9 cakes

Keys to Success

■ *Home-made butter puff pastry will achieve a superior quality. Use bought puff pastry only as a last resort.*

■ *If you don't have Armagnac, feel free to use Cognac, Cointreau or another liqueur. The important thing is to allow the fruit to soak up the liqueur.*

■ *Allowing the puff pastry to rest during the rolling process and once the Eccles Cakes are assembled will result in an even, round shape.*

■ *A hot oven will ensure a crisp, flaky pastry, but take care that the sugar doesn't start to burn too soon: the result will be a dark brown colour on the outside and doughy pastry inside.*

Lemon and Blueberry Polenta Cake

A delicious gluten-free cake, made with polenta instead of wheat flour. It's best eaten within a couple of days after baking. This will not be difficult!

Batter

225g butter, softened
½ teaspoon pure vanilla essence
225g caster sugar
3 eggs
150g ground almonds
200g finely ground polenta
½ teaspoon baking powder
juice and zest of 3 lemons, slightly warmed
200g blueberries or other berries, fresh or frozen

■ Preheat the oven to 175°C.

Beat the butter, vanilla and sugar together, preferably in an electric mixer with a beater attachment. Stop when the butter and sugar just begin to change colour and the mixture is light and fluffy. Add the eggs one by one, beating well between each addition to ensure that the mixture does not curdle.

Sift the ground almonds, polenta and baking powder together. Add to the creamy batter, along with the lemon juice and zest, and fold in gently. Lastly, add the berries and fold in until evenly distributed.

Place the batter into a lightly greased spring-release cake tin lined with baking paper. Bake for 1 hour. Test whether baking is complete by inserting a skewer in the centre: if it comes out clean, remove the cake from the oven.

Allow the cake to cool for 10–15 minutes before removing it from the tin. Make the Lemon Icing while you wait for the cake to cool completely.

Lemon Icing

300g icing sugar
zest of 1 lemon
4 tablespoons lemon juice

■ Sift the icing sugar into a bowl and add the lemon zest and juice. Stir until you achieve a thick, spreadable icing. When the cake is completely cool, spread the icing on top and allow it to run down the sides ever so slightly.

Lemon Julienne

rind of 2 lemons
100g sugar
100ml water

■ Cut paper-thin strips of lemon rind and poach until soft (approximately 5 minutes) in a sugar solution made from the sugar and water. Drain the strips and dry them with a paper towel before decorating the icing with them.

■ Makes 1 x 20cm round cake

Keys to Success

■ *The polenta needed for this recipe has the texture of very finely ground breadcrumbs. Do not use instant polenta.*

■ *When folding in the berries, take care not to over-mix or the batter will discolour.*

■ *By greasing the cake tin lightly and lining it with baking paper, you can insulate the cake during its time in the oven. This prevents over-baking on or near the surface.*

■ *The Lemon Icing and Lemon Julienne can be prepared in advance.*

■ *If the icing is too liquid, add more icing sugar. If it is too thick, add a few more drops of lemon juice.*

Almond, Basil and Citrus Cake

This moist, gluten-free cake is enriched by basil and lime. Forward planning is needed: it's not a difficult or labour-intensive recipe (it's as easy as ABC) but, to maximise the flavour, you will need to make the cake over three days. It will be well worth that effort. Serve with whipped cream for dessert, or accompany with tea or coffee.

Citrus Purée

2 medium oranges
4 small limes
1 cup shredded fresh basil leaves

■ Make this on day one.
   Wash the oranges and limes. Place them in a saucepan, cover with water and bring to the boil. Simmer for 1½ hours, with the lid partly off to prevent the pan from boiling dry.
   Discard the water. Quarter the oranges and limes and remove the pips. Place in a food processor and purée. Pour into a bowl and stir the basil through. Cover with plastic wrap and refrigerate overnight.

Batter

15g baking powder
310g ground almonds
400g eggs (approximately 8 eggs)
310g caster sugar
350–400g Citrus Purée

■ Make this on day two. Preheat the oven to 170°C.
   Mix the baking powder and ground almonds together. Using a separate bowl and a hand-held whisk, whisk the eggs and sugar together gently, until just combined. Using a wooden spoon, add the Citrus Purée and the dry ingredients. Mix gently until well combined.
   Pour the mixture into a greased and baking paper-lined cake tin with a removable base. Bake for 80–90 minutes.
   Remove the cake from the oven and cool overnight in the tin.
   On day three, remove the baking paper and place the cake on a rack.

Apricot Glaze and Pistachios

150ml water
300g apricot jam
75g green-skinned pistachios, cut into slivers

■ Place the water and jam in a saucepan and bring to the boil, stirring. Strain through a sieve and use while hot. You may need to warm the glaze from time to time.
   Using a pastry brush, brush the top and sides of the cake with the glaze, coating evenly to achieve a glossy finish. Decorate the top of the cake with a ring of pistachios around the edge.

■ Makes 1 x 22cm round cake

Keys to Success

■ One quantity of prepared Citrus Purée should weigh 350–400g. Take care not to add more to the batter, or the baked cake will be soggy and too dense.

■ Another way to prevent your cake from being soggy, sunken and overly dense is to check that baking is complete before removing it from the oven. The cake is ready when an inserted skewer comes out clean.

■ Dean prefers to weigh eggs (breaking them first) for this recipe; it is much more accurate than simply counting.

■ A hand-whisk is ideal for mixing the sugar and eggs: you are less likely to over-mix or whisk too much air into the batter.

■ Cooling the cake overnight enhances the flavour. Covering it with plastic wrap at this time will keep it moist.

German Chocolate Cake

In 1947, a Texas newspaper published a home cook's chocolate cake recipe using a chocolate bar invented by Sam German. That was the first of numerous 'German Chocolate Cakes' — many of them (including this one) now made without chocolate bars at all. The main thing they have in common is that they are sweet . . . very sweet!

Batter

> 40g cocoa powder
> 200g standard flour
> ½ teaspoon baking soda
> pinch of salt
> 115g butter
> 200g sugar
> 115g light brown sugar
> 1½ teaspoons pure vanilla essence
> 2 large eggs, beaten
> 200ml buttermilk

■ Preheat the oven to 175°C. Sift the cocoa, flour, baking soda and salt together. Set aside.

Beat the butter, sugars and vanilla together until creamy, light and smooth, preferably in an electric mixer fitted with a beater attachment. Pour the eggs in gradually and incorporate them, on a low speed. Add a third of the buttermilk, then a third of the dry ingredients. Repeat until all the buttermilk and dry ingredients are incorporated.

Line a lightly greased spring-release 20cm cake-tin with baking paper. Scrape the batter in. Bake for approximately 80 minutes while you make the Caramel Icing.

Remove the cake from the oven when a skewer inserted in the centre of the cake comes out clean. Rest the cake for a few minutes, then remove it from the tin. Take off the baking paper and cool the cake completely before icing it.

Caramel Icing

> 265g sweetened condensed milk
> 55g butter, at room temperature
> 40g golden syrup
> 25g soft brown sugar
> ¼ teaspoon pure vanilla essence
> 75g shredded coconut, lightly toasted
> 75g pecans, chopped and lightly toasted

■ Measure the condensed milk, butter, golden syrup, sugar and vanilla into a bowl. Cook them in the microwave for 1 minute on high. Stir thoroughly. Return to the microwave and cook for 30 seconds on high, then stir thoroughly again. Repeat the process four more times for 30 seconds each time. Stir in the coconut and pecans.

The icing should be thick and spreadable. Allow it to cool and spread it on top of the cooled cake.

■ Makes 1 x 20cm round cake

Keys to Success

■ *Baking paper will insulate the cake during its time in the oven, preventing over-baking on or near the surface.*

■ *Watch when making the Caramel Icing, as this will thicken quickly in the microwave.*

■ *The icing can be made in a heavy-based saucepan over very gentle heat. Stir constantly and remove from the heat when it becomes thick and spreadable, approximately 6 minutes.*

■ *Allow both the cake and the icing to cool completely before you apply the icing, otherwise it will not set.*

Courgette, Carrot and Poppy-Seed Loaf

A great variation on one of New Zealand's favourites: the carrot cake. This sweet loaf is enhanced by courgette and poppy seeds and is topped with a delicious creamy icing.

Batter

185g standard flour
½ teaspoon baking soda
¼ teaspoon baking powder
1 teaspoon cinnamon
⅛ teaspoon ground allspice
¼ teaspoon ground ginger
¼ teaspoon salt
1 large egg, at room temperature
170g caster sugar
110ml vegetable oil
4 drops pure vanilla essence
60g courgettes, grated
60g carrots, grated
10g poppy seeds
½ tablespoon lemon zest

■ Preheat the oven to 180ºC. Sift the flour, baking soda, baking powder, spices and salt into a bowl and set aside.

Whisk the egg and sugar together until thick and creamy — preferably in an electric mixer, using the whisk attachment. Check for readiness by drizzling a little of the mixture onto the remainder. The drizzled mixture should stay on top for about 10 seconds before being absorbed.

With the mixer on a low speed, slowly pour the oil into the egg and sugar, mixing until it is well incorporated. A mayonnaise-like consistency should result.

Add the vanilla, courgettes, carrots, poppy seeds and lemon zest and mix for a few seconds. Gently fold the dry ingredients in until they are evenly combined. Line a loaf tin with baking paper, pour the mixture in and bake for 40–45 minutes.

Remove the loaf from the oven and leave to cool for 5–10 minutes before turning out onto a cooling rack (this is a good opportunity to make the icing). Allow to cool completely before applying the icing.

Lemon Cream-Cheese Icing and Cinnamon Dusting

75g cream cheese
70g butter, softened
145g icing sugar, sifted
1 tablespoon lemon zest
1 tablespoon lemon juice
cinnamon, for dusting

■ Beat the cream cheese, butter, icing sugar, lemon zest and juice together on a moderate speed until the icing is white and fluffy. Ice the loaf and decorate the icing by patting it with the back of a knife. Dust the top of the icing lightly with cinnamon.

■ Makes 1 x 19cm x 9cm x 6.5cm deep loaf

Keys to Success

■ *Instead of using baking paper, you can brush the tin with butter and dust with flour. This will result in a darker crust.*

■ *To test whether the loaf is baked, either press it lightly with a fingertip (the surface should spring back, showing no sign of your touch), or insert a skewer into the centre (if it comes out clean, the loaf is ready).*

■ *The icing can be made in advance and refrigerated in a covered bowl for 2–3 days until needed.*

Fresh Ginger and Honey Nut Loaf

The aroma of fresh ginger and the sweetness of honey . . . this moist, hazelnut-flavoured loaf is manna from heaven. Cut a slice, spread it thinly with butter and drizzle with liquid honey. Delicious!

3cm piece fresh root ginger, peeled
115g honey
115g golden syrup
50g butter, softened
2 small eggs
3 tablespoons milk
¾ teaspoon baking soda
140g standard flour
¾ teaspoon ground cinnamon
¾ teaspoon ground allspice
100g hazelnuts, chopped and lightly toasted
2 tablespoons honey, for glazing

■ Preheat the oven to 170ºC.

Grate the ginger onto a double thickness of muslin and roll the muslin up tightly. Over a bowl, wring the juice out of the ginger, getting as much juice as possible. Reserve the juice and discard the pulp.

Beat the honey, golden syrup and butter together on a moderate speed until the mixture is light in colour, approximately 3 minutes. Add the eggs and the ginger juice. Mix on a low speed until combined, approximately 1 minute.

Warm the milk to blood temperature and stir in the baking soda. Add to the batter and mix on a low speed until combined, approximately 30 seconds.

Sift the dry ingredients together into a bowl and add the hazelnuts. Using a spatula, fold the dry ingredients into the batter, mixing well and ensuring that there are no lumps of flour left. The batter should be runny.

Line a lightly greased loaf tin with baking paper. Pour the mixture in. Bake in the middle of the oven for 40–50 minutes.

In a saucepan or microwave, melt the second measure of honey gently over a low heat. While the loaf is still hot, brush the top with the melted honey.

Allow the loaf to cool, remove it from the tin and remove the paper. Slice the loaf and serve it with a thin spread of butter and a drizzle of honey.

■ Makes 1 x 19cm x 9cm x 6.5cm deep loaf

Keys to Success

■ Using freshly grated ginger really does make a difference and is well worth the effort.

■ If you don't like hazelnuts, feel free to omit them or substitute other nuts of your choice.

■ Don't be tempted to add more flour to the runny batter. This consistency results in a pleasingly moist quality in the baked loaf.

■ To check that the loaf is baked, insert a skewer into the centre. If it comes out clean, the loaf is ready.

Spiced Dairy-Free Fruit and Nut Loaf

Health-conscious consumers often look for recipes that are completely dairy-free. This easy-to-prepare cake is packed with walnuts, cashews, almonds, dates and figs. The dense texture, almost like pumpernickel, makes it chewy and moist. Top with a large spoonful of your favourite preserve!

Batter

100g pitted dates, chopped
100g dried figs, chopped
250ml soy milk
¼ cup liquid honey
1 teaspoon all-vegetable margarine
100g self-raising flour
60g wholemeal flour
1 teaspoon cinnamon
¼ teaspoon ground cloves
200g raw cashews, roughly chopped
100g blanched almonds, roughly chopped
100g walnuts, roughly chopped
all-vegetable cooking spray, for spraying
35g flaked almonds, for topping

■ Preheat the oven to 180°C.

Place the dates, figs, soy milk, honey and margarine in a food processor. Blend until the dates and figs are evenly dispersed through the liquid. Transfer the mixture to a large bowl. Add the flours and spices, mixing with a wooden spoon until well combined. Using a spatula, fold the nuts through until evenly distributed, taking care not to over-mix the batter.

Pour the mixture into a non-stick loaf tin lightly sprayed with cooking spray. Smooth the top, and sprinkle evenly with the flaked almonds. Bake for 1 hour, until golden-brown and firm to the touch.

Apricot Glaze

3 tablespoons water
100g apricot jam

■ Make this just before you remove the loaf from the oven — or make it in advance and reheat it when required.

Place the water and jam in a saucepan and bring to the boil, stirring. Strain through a sieve.

Remove the loaf from the oven, take it out of the tin, place on a cooling rack and brush with apricot glaze while both the glaze and the loaf are hot.

■ Makes 1 x 19cm x 9cm x 6.5cm deep loaf

Keys to Success

■ *If you don't have wholemeal flour, you can use standard flour.*

■ *Feel free to substitute other nuts of your choice for the cashews, almonds and walnuts. You may even replace some of the nuts with candied fruits such as pineapple, ginger and apricots.*

■ *Toast the nuts lightly if you want to enhance the flavour: spread them out on a baking tray lined with baking paper and bake at 150°C until light amber in colour, approximately 10 minutes. Don't over-toast, as this will result in a dry loaf. Nuts, being dense, continue cooking for a short time after you remove them from the oven.*

■ *Using a food processor to combine the dates, figs, margarine and liquid ingredients will ensure that they are blended well.*

Chocolate Almond Macaroons

Dean has wanted to know how to perfect these bite-sized macaroons ever since he discovered them at Jean-Luc Poujuran's Parisian pâtisserie. Now he has the recipe from BakeMark Ingredients France's Export Pastry Chef, Olivier Hutt, Dean is happy! The macaroons are perfect as petit fours or after-dinner treats.

Batter

125g ground almonds
210g icing sugar
15g cocoa powder
100g egg whites (approximately 3 whites)
25g caster sugar
⅛ teaspoon cream of tartar

■ Sift the ground almonds, icing sugar and cocoa together. (You may have to use your hand to push the almonds through the sieve.) Combine the ingredients well and set aside.

Whisk the egg whites, caster sugar and cream of tartar on a high speed, preferably using an electric mixer fitted with a whisk attachment. Stop when the mixture holds stiff peaks. Add the dry ingredients. Using a wooden spoon or spatula, mix them in until a thick paste has formed.

Place the mixture in a piping bag fitted with a small plain piping tube about ½cm in diameter. Pipe small bulbs of macaroon mixture about 1½cm in diameter onto a baking tray lined with baking paper, allowing a gap of at least 2cm between each one.

Lift the tray up and bang it on the bench a couple of times to allow the mixture to settle and spread a little. Leave the unbaked macaroons at room temperature for 45 minutes to form a skin while you preheat the oven to 200°C.

Bake for 8–10 minutes until the macaroons have risen and spread slightly. Remove from the oven and allow to cool completely (you can make the Ganache while waiting). Gently peel each macaroon off the baking paper.

Ganache

100g cream
200g dark chocolate, finely chopped
2 teaspoons Amaretto liqueur or rum (optional)

■ Place the cream in a saucepan and gently bring to the boil. Remove from the heat and add the chocolate and Amaretto. Stir with a wooden spoon until all the chocolate has melted. Place the mixture in a bowl, cover and leave out at room temperature to cool (do not put it in the fridge). Beat the ganache with a wooden spoon until it changes colour and becomes lighter in texture.

Assembly

■ Place the ganache in a piping bag fitted with a small plain piping tube. Pipe a dot of ganache onto the base of a macaroon and then sandwich with another macaroon, base to base. Continue until all the macaroons have been sandwiched. Allow the ganache to set before eating, if you can wait that long!

■ **Makes 40 sandwiched macaroons**

Keys to Success

■ *All utensils need to be completely clean and free of any traces of fat or grease. Wash them beforehand in hot soapy water, rinse them well (also in hot water) and dry with a paper towel.*

■ *Feel free to make the ganache in advance and keep it until required. Ensure it is firm, lightly whipped and at room temperature before you use it.*

■ *Make sure the almonds are very finely ground. If they are coarse, place them in a food processor with the icing sugar and blend until a fine powder has formed.*

■ *When mixing the dry ingredients in, don't worry about losing the air bubbles you have just created: too much air in the mixture will cause the individual macaroons to puff up in the oven.*

Classic Shortbread

Shortbread is a culinary classic. There are so many recipes it's hard to know which one is the best, but this is Dean's all-time favourite. Rice flour strengthens the shortbread and gives it a wonderful crispness.

300g butter, softened
170g caster sugar
400g standard flour
20g cornflour
40g rice flour
pinch of salt
caster sugar, for sprinkling (optional)

■ Preheat the oven to 180°C.

Cream the butter and sugar until light and fluffy, preferably using an electric mixer. Sift the flour, cornflour, rice flour and salt together.

Add half the dry ingredients to the butter and sugar, and cream again until light and fluffy.

On a low speed, blend in the rest of the dry ingredients until the mixture comes away from the sides of the mixing bowl and gathers as one mass of dough.

On a lightly floured bench, roll the dough out to 1.5cm thick. Cut into the desired shapes. Place on a baking tray lined with a double thickness of baking paper. Prick with a fork.

Bake for 10–20 minutes (depending on the size of the pieces) or until it is a very pale golden colour.

Remove from the oven and sprinkle immediately with caster sugar if desired.

■ Makes approximately 36 rectangular shortbread biscuits

Keys to Success

■ Countless ingredients can be added to this basic dough to vary the flavour. Experiment with toasted walnut pieces, flaked almonds, lavender, crystallised ginger, dried cranberries or glacé cherries. Add them after you blend in the dry ingredients.

■ Soft butter will help to achieve a light and creamy mixture.

■ Rice flour, which creates the crisp quality, is available from most supermarkets or specialty stores. If you don't have any, simply replace it with standard flour.

■ The dough can be made in advance. Roll the unbaked shortbread into logs, approximately 5cm in diameter. Wrap in plastic wrap and place in the refrigerator or freezer for 2–3 hours until firm all the way through. Use as needed, cutting 1.5cm-thick slices in the quantity required, warming to room temperature before baking.

■ For visual appeal, you can not only shape your unbaked shortbread using cookie cutters but also press it. The long association of shortbread with Scotland means that the most popular design is a large round biscuit (using one quantity of shortbread mixture), featuring a thistle impression that is made with a shortbread press or mould. The baking time for a single large biscuit is about the same as for individual small pieces.

■ A double thickness of baking paper insulates the shortbread base from the heat, preventing it from turning dark brown. A good shortbread is pale gold all over.

Oatmeal Parmesan Biscuits

These savoury biscuits are great eaten with cheese and a selection of fresh fruits such as pears, apples, grapes and apricots. The nutty flavour of the sesame seeds combines well with the Parmesan and the slightly sweet oatmeal.

125g medium-ground oatmeal
60g standard flour
60g wholemeal flour
¼ teaspoon baking soda
½ teaspoon salt
½ teaspoon soft brown sugar
40g Parmesan cheese, finely grated
125g butter, chilled and cut into 1cm cubes
½ beaten egg
sesame seeds, for decoration

■ Preheat the oven to 180ºC.

Place all the dry ingredients, including the Parmesan, in a large bowl. Rub the butter in with your fingers until the mixture resembles breadcrumbs. Add the egg. Using your hands, combine the ingredients to form a soft dough.

On a lightly floured bench, roll the dough out to 3–4mm thick. Using a 5cm round biscuit-cutter, cut biscuits out.

Dip the cut edges into water and very gently roll the edges in the sesame seeds so they are covered with seeds.

Line a baking tray with baking paper, place the biscuits on the tray and bake for 8–10 minutes until they turn a golden, sandy colour and are firm to touch. The biscuits will become crisp when cool.

■ Makes 30–36 biscuits

Keys to Success

■ If you cannot buy a medium-ground oatmeal, blend rolled oats in a food processor until a medium-ground oatmeal is formed.

■ If you dislike a cheesy flavour, simply omit the Parmesan.

■ Cold butter makes it easier to create a breadcrumb texture.

■ If the dough is too firm, add more egg.

■ To apply the sesame seeds easily, hold a stack of cut biscuits vertically between your thumb and forefinger. Roll them like a wheel, first in a shallow water-bath and then in the sesame seeds.

■ The dough can be made in advance and kept in the fridge for 1–2 days. Allow the dough to warm up a little and rework it to soften before rolling it out.

■ Don't over-bake these little biscuits; this will make them too dry.

Whole-Wheat Crackers

These moreish crackers are really savoury, with lingering Asian flavours that are perfect with any pâté or hummus. Once baked and crisp, they can be stored in an airtight container for up to one month — if they last that long!

Spice Mixture

3 teaspoons sesame seeds
1½ teaspoons anise seeds, slightly bruised
¾ teaspoon nigella seeds or black onion seeds
¾ teaspoon sea salt flakes
scant ½ teaspoon chilli powder

■ Stir all the ingredients together in a bowl and set aside.

Dough

100g standard flour
100g wholemeal flour
½ teaspoon salt
1½ teaspoons olive oil
1 small red chilli, seeds removed, chopped
* very finely*
120ml warm water (quantity approximate)

■ Place the flours, salt, oil and chilli in a bowl. Slowly add the water, mixing until you achieve a firm dough. If the mixture is too dry, add 1–2 tablespoons more water. If it is too sticky, add 2–3 tablespoons more flour.

Tip the dough ball out onto the bench and knead by hand for 5 minutes, resting every couple of minutes. The resulting dough should be smooth but still firm. Place the dough in a lightly floured bowl, cover it with plastic wrap and leave for 30 minutes.

On a lightly floured bench, cut the dough into five equal pieces. Mould each into a ball, cover with plastic wrap and rest the dough again for 20 minutes. Meanwhile, preheat the oven to 250°C.

Roll one dough ball out on the bench to a thin, round circle approximately 20cm in diameter. Place this on a baking tray lined with baking paper. Lightly brush the dough surface with water and sprinkle about ½ teaspoon of the prepared Spice Mixture on top.

Brush the edge of a large sharp knife or pizza-cutter blade with olive oil. Cut the prepared dough circle into eight equally sized triangular wedges (there is no need to separate them out). Bake for 3–5 minutes until the crackers are golden-brown. Remove them from the tray and break them into the wedges.

Cool the tray while you repeat the rolling, seasoning and cutting procedures for each dough ball in turn. Bake as above.

■ Makes 40 triangular crackers

Keys to Success

■ *Use a mortar and pestle or a rolling pin and chopping board to bruise the anise seeds.*

■ *These crackers are made with a similar procedure to that of a typical bread dough, although they are yeast-free. Refer to pages 44-45 in the Breads chapter for advice on kneading.*

■ *If adding extra water to the dough, don't be tempted to add too much (even though it will make the kneading easier). The dough needs to be firm.*

■ *Avoid hurrying when rolling the dough balls out to 20cm circles. By allowing the dough to rest several times during this process, you will make it easier.*

■ *If you brush your blade with oil before cutting the rolled dough circles, there is no need to separate the crackers further or to spread them across the tray before you bake them.*

Chocolate, Cognac and Pecan Truffle Cookies

Filled with pecans, real chocolate and a hint of Cognac, these cookies are great on their own as a treat or served as a petit four with coffee after dinner.

60g butter, softened
185g brown sugar
1½ tablespoons Cognac
zest of ½ orange
1 egg
30g dark chocolate, melted
1 tablespoon milk
170g standard flour
1 tablespoon cocoa powder
1 teaspoon baking powder
50g pecans, chopped
icing sugar, for coating

■ Beat the butter, sugar, Cognac and orange zest until light and fluffy. Beat in the egg, then stir in the melted chocolate and milk.

Sift the flour, cocoa and baking powder into the mixture. Combine well using a wooden spoon.

Stir in the pecans until evenly distributed. Refrigerate the batter for at least 3 hours.

Preheat the oven to 180°C.

Roll tablespoons of the mixture into balls, then roll each ball in the icing sugar to coat each one evenly.

Place the cookies well apart on a baking tray lined with baking paper. Bake for 20–25 minutes or until slightly firm to the touch.

Remove from the oven and leave on the tray for 3–4 minutes. Place on a cooling rack.

■ Makes approximately 20 cookies

Keys to Success

■ If you don't have Cognac, substitute 1 teaspoon of pure vanilla essence and double the quantity of milk.

■ Leaving the mixture to firm up in the refrigerator will make it easier to shape the cookies into balls and coat them in icing sugar. If you can't wait 3 hours, be very gentle when shaping the cookies.

■ To make smaller petit-four-size cookies, use a good rounded teaspoon of mixture for each ball.

■ Avoid over-baking these cookies; otherwise the icing sugar will begin to caramelise and the contrast of white sugar and darker batter will be lost.

■ Note that dense items such as biscuits continue cooking for a short time after you remove them from the oven.

Kahlúa Walnut Chocolate Truffles

There's no baking involved in this mouth-watering recipe but it takes a little time and effort. High-quality truffles don't grow on trees — or even underneath them!

130g milk chocolate, preferably Belgian
130g white chocolate
80ml cream
20g unsalted butter
35ml Kahlúa liqueur
100g walnuts, chopped quite finely
icing sugar, to powder hands
350g milk or white chocolate, for coating

■ Break or chop both 130g measures of chocolate into small pieces and set aside. In a heavy-based saucepan, heat the cream and butter until they reach 90°C or just below boiling point. Remove the saucepan from the heat and add the broken chocolate, Kahlúa and walnuts. Stir until the chocolate has melted.

Pour the truffle mixture into a container lined with greaseproof paper. Refrigerate for 1–2 hours, until firm.

Use a teaspoon to scoop out heaped teaspoons of truffle mixture. Powder the palms of your hands with icing sugar and roll the mixture into balls. Place the truffles on a tray lined with greaseproof paper and refrigerate for approximately 1 hour to set.

Melt the last measure of chocolate (milk or white). Coat your palms in chocolate and roll the truffles in the chocolate, making sure each truffle is covered with a thin, even coating of chocolate. Alternatively, place each truffle on a chocolate-dipping fork, dip into the melted chocolate and tap to remove excess chocolate. You can repeat this dipping and coating process if you want a thicker layer of chocolate.

Return the chocolate-coated truffles to the greaseproof paper to set. Store in a cool, dark place. Always serve truffles at room temperature.

■ Makes approximately 50 truffles (heaped-teaspoon-size)

Keys to Success

■ *Top-quality chocolate is recommended but not essential. Buy the best you can afford.*

■ *Feel free to use chocolate couverture for the chocolate coating. See the notes on tempering chocolate in the Ingredients section (page 144).*

■ *When you initially pour the truffle mixture out, you may like to use a 20cm square tin or plastic container.*

Pistachio and Chocolate Meringues

Dean first spotted meringues like these in London's Baker and Spice bakery. They seemed to be the size of small mountains, and he wondered who would buy such a huge meringue. Of course, he bought one . . . It tasted exceptional, lighter than light — so he decided to try making them at home.

115g egg whites (approximately 4 whites)
225g caster sugar
150g chocolate, broken into pieces
80g green-skinned pistachios, cut into slivers
   or roughly chopped

■ Preheat the oven to 150ºC. Heat a pan of water to a low simmer. Put the egg whites and sugar into a glass or metal bowl and set it over the pan. Stir until the sugar dissolves and the mixture is warm to the touch.

Whisk the mixture until it is thick and cool, forming stiff peaks. This should take approximately 15 minutes with an electric mixer and whisk attachment.

Using a large metal spoon, fold the chocolate and about three-quarters of the pistachios into the mixture. Reserve the rest of the pistachios for decoration.

Line a baking tray with baking paper. Using your largest serving spoon, drop six large dollops of the mixture onto the tray. Sprinkle each meringue with the reserved pistachios and place the tray in the oven. Turn the oven off, leaving the door partly open, to dry the meringues out. Leave overnight or until the oven is completely cold.

Serve the meringues with your favourite ice-cream, fresh fruit, whipped cream and seasonal berries — or simply enjoy them on their own.

■ **Makes 6 large meringues**

Keys to Success

■ *The hours of drying out are essential to the success of this dish, so it's not one to make when you need instant gratification.*

■ *With meringues, it is especially important that all utensils are completely clean and free of any traces of fat or grease. Wash them beforehand in hot soapy water, rinse them well (also in hot water) and dry with a paper towel.*

■ *Dean prefers to weigh egg whites for this recipe; it is much more accurate than simply counting.*

■ *When warming the egg whites and sugar, avoid heating the water to a rolling boil as this will cook the egg whites.*

■ *Don't worry if the meringues crack when drying out; this adds to their visual appeal.*

Equipment

The reality of baking at home is that you don't need any specialist baking tools. Some years ago, all that any creditable baker (let alone home baker) had was a large mixing bowl, a few cups and spoons, a solid rolling-pin, a few knives, a whisk, an oven and — most importantly — a good eye and a pair of strong yet sensitive hands.

■ The following are the basic tools of the trade, and the list is not so very different from the one above. Wherever Dean's baking work takes him, these tools are usually available in one form or another. Many, many other pieces of equipment can be used — and some are suggested in the pages of this book — but there is no need for baking to be complex: keep things simple!

How simple can baking be? This bakery in a suburb of Shanghai, pictured left, has a small, run-down mixer, bench, human hands and a tandoori-style oven (in the foreground) to make a typical Chinese spring onion and egg flat bread.

Your Hands

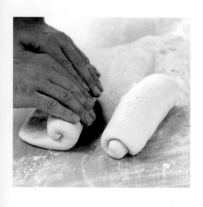

■ These are the two most important pieces of equipment for your baking toolbox. Your hands must be strong and firm, yet gentle and sensitive. They need to be able to knead. At the same time, they must be light and delicate enough to gently fold and lift the softest of flours through a perfectly aerated batter.

You need a good sense of temperature and consistency when using your hands. By repeating a recipe, you will develop the 'baker's feel'. This means discerning when a dough is fully mixed, elastic, smooth and silky to the touch. It means knowing when to stop folding the flour into a delicate, light-as-air sponge or when to put a loaf of bread in the oven. It also means knowing when your product is under-baked, perfectly baked or over-baked.

Theoretically, you can use a bread-making machine for the kneading process with bread recipes in this book. However, it is better to knead by hand because of the sensitivity you develop while constantly monitoring your dough. For more thoughts on bread-making machines, see page 42.

Scrapers, mixers, spoons and knives certainly have their place. All too often, though, home bakers use such tools to distance themselves from the dough or batter they are working with, for fear that their hands will get messy and sticky. Dean's message is: get right into it, and don't underestimate the importance of your hands in baking.

Electric Mixer

■ Do you need a big, expensive mixer? Dean still has the hand-me-down from his grandmother and for the amount he uses it, it's not worth buying an expensive mixer, much as he would like one. He makes all the breads, cakes and pastries by hand, and the only time he really needs an electric mixer is when he wants to mix a sponge or make an icing that needs to be light, fluffy and airy. However, a mixer can also help on days when you lack energy, as baking can be a strenuous physical workout.

Food processors are not suitable for kneading firm doughs or whipping air into a delicate sponge mixture, as their real strength and purpose lie in their cutting actions. Processors are great for creating the purées and pastes often used in baking.

Scales

■ If you plan to bake from simple raw ingredients, do yourself a favour and buy a good set of digital scales: it's well worth the investment. If a recipe calls for 100g of sugar, that's what is needed — not 115 or 150 grams. Alternatively, use a good set of balance scales with the ability to weigh in 5g increments.

Mixing Bowls

■ It is useful to have an abundance of bowls of different sizes, ranging from a very large earthenware bowl for mixing pastry and doughs to small glass bowls in which to keep individual ingredients ready and waiting for combination in the chosen recipe.

Baking Tins and Trays

■ You can have a baking tin or mould for every occasion, but the following are the basic essentials:

■ **10 small tart tins, approximately 8cm in diameter** — used for creating individual sweet or savoury tarts. These are usually fluted.

■ **25cm and 20cm flan tins with removable bases** — used for large sweet and savoury flans.

■ **a 20cm round cake tin with a removable base and high sides** — essential for any round cake or sponge.

■ **two good solid baking trays** — the kind that has been around for a while, well used and strong (won't bend with a heavy tart on it).

■ **a baking mat** — this is an essential professional baking tool that allows you to bake anything on it without sticking. Baking mats of commercial quality are available from all good cook shops. Don't cut on the mat, or it will have cuts all over it. If you take good care of it, you will have it for years. Baking paper, mentioned throughout this book, can always be used instead of a baking mat. Often the same sheet can be reused before you throw it away.

■ **two mini-muffin pans** — tiny muffins and Christmas fruit mince tarts made in these mini-muffin pans are very cute. Once you make a batch of muffins in them, there's no turning back.

■ **a Swiss-roll or slice tray** — these have short sides that make them ideal for a variety of products and tasks, from baking the perfect brownie to toasting nuts.

■ **a loaf tin** — for baking the traditional cake-type loaf or a 500g loaf of bread.

■ **a baking stone** — to provide insulation and solid heat when baking bread, resulting in more even baking than a metal oven tray. When you first receive your baking stone, condition it in the oven at a low temperature for several hours.

Knives, Scrapers, Whisks and Other Small Utensils

■ The knives, scrapers, cutters, teaspoons, measuring cups, wooden spoons and whisks that you use are very much a personal choice. Over the years of baking, you will no doubt collect many different pieces of smaller equipment, some of which will become your favourites.

Small utensils mentioned in this book include:

■ **dough scraper or cutter** — a rectangular piece of stainless steel with a rolled or wooden handle and a sharp edge. Uses include dividing or cutting dough and scraping excess flour off the bench.

■ **pastry brush** — a versatile tool whose uses include glazing and dusting.

■ **palette knife** — a thin, flexible, round-ended, blunt knife used for spreading icing and other substances onto cakes and other baked items.

Dough Cloths and Covers

■ Covering your dough, which after all is a living organism, is like tucking yourself up in bed with a cosy blanket. The dough is covered with a light cloth, such as a tea-towel or a piece of strong plastic wrap, to prevent the dough from getting cold and the yeast from working at a much slower pace. There is another vital reason for this practice: to prevent the unbaked dough from forming a dry skin or crust.

You can also use a heavier cloth, made from canvas or Belgian linen, which is known as a proving cloth or a couche in French. This is dusted well with flour, then gathered around the shape of the dough piece to help hold the shape of the loaves or baguettes, preventing them from drying out on the sides and base during long proving and fermentation times.

Thermometers

■ A long-stemmed digital thermometer works well for reading dough and ingredient temperatures. You may also want an oven thermometer, as ovens (especially domestic ones) can have temperature variations as much as 20°C.

Ovens

■ There is no need for the home baker to invest thousands of dollars in a state-of-the-art oven; you can just make a few adjustments to your existing oven. For example, to create steam in your oven, you can either spray the oven walls with warm water from a spray bottle or simply toss some ice cubes into a preheated baking dish at the bottom of the oven. This creates a steamy, humid environment for your bread to bake in. There is no need to do this for pastries, tarts, biscuits or cakes.

Before placing anything in the oven to bake, always check that it is set at the correct temperature and has reached that temperature.

All recipes in this book are based on a standard oven (without a fan). If using a fan-assisted oven, reduce the temperature by 10–15°C and pay close attention as the baking time will also be reduced.

Ingredients

All the basic ingredients of baking are simple, natural products. They can be found in mainstream supermarkets and food stores. Keep your ingredients in a cool, dark, dry cupboard or drawer, and always use them as fresh as possible.

Yeast

Origin: yeast is a fungus; a living single-cell organism that is oval in shape and can only be seen under a microscope. It exists almost everywhere, which is why bakers can make bread based on a flour-and-water starter that has had contact with fresh air. The species of yeast used by commercial bakers and brewers is *Saccharomyces cerevisiae*, although the two industries use different strains of this.

Claims to Fame: yeast has been used for millennia in the making of bread, beer and wine. The Egyptians were the first to discover how to make yeast-raised breads, between 2000 and 3000 BC. It was only in the nineteenth century that Louis Pasteur confirmed the fermentation role of live yeast in wine and beer.

Saccharomyces cerevisiae is responsible for volume in bread, buns, rolls, croissants, Danish pastries and similar products.

Because yeast lacks chlorophyll, which enables green plants to make their own food, it feeds on sugar from nature (including fruit and grain). In dough, yeast brings about fermentation, by breaking sugars down into carbon dioxide and alcohol. This gas produces the rising (often called leavening) action in yeast-raised products. The alcohol evaporates completely during and immediately after baking.

For yeast to produce carbon dioxide and alcohol, it needs:

- time to ferment and produce carbon dioxide;
- moisture to survive and grow;
- warmth — the ideal temperature is 28–32°C;
- food — a source to feed upon, from which carbon dioxide will be produced.

Without these conditions, the yeast cells will die and baking will fail.

For more information on how yeast works in the bread-making process, see the two 'How It Works' sections in the Breads chapter, pages 42 and 52.

Varieties:

■ **Fresh Yeast (also called Compressed Yeast)** — all recipes in this book call for fresh yeast, and this is certainly preferable. It is difficult to get, but you may find that a local bakery is willing to part with some, or a select few specialty stores may sell it. The shelf life is very limited, and fresh yeast should not be frozen. Store it in the refrigerator and use as soon as possible, discarding any yeast that remains after the use-by date.

■ **Active Dry Yeast** — can be purchased from your local supermarket. It has an excellent shelf life unopened. When using active dry yeast in place of fresh yeast, use two-thirds less. For instance, substitute 5g of active dry yeast for 15g fresh yeast.

■ **Wild Yeast** — various strains live in the air around us and are used in sourdough or levain starters.

Water

Composition: hydrogen and oxygen.

Claims to Fame: "a colourless, transparent, odourless liquid which forms the seas, lakes, rivers and rain and is the basis of the fluids of living organisms," says the *Oxford Dictionary of English*.

Water is a key ingredient in baking, in particular bread-making. It is needed to form the gluten network and give consistency to dough and is essential to fermentation. It distributes and combines other ingredients and it is absorbed by the starch, making the baked product digestible. Water also helps to distribute heat through the mixture during baking.

Use water that is as fresh as possible. In bread doughs, warm water (20–25°C) is usually used but chilled water is sometimes called for.

Wheat Flour

Origin: the cereal wheat was originally a wild grass. Evidence suggests that Mesopotamia and the Tigris River and Euphrates River valleys, in the Middle East, were the first places where wheat grew — nearly 10,000 years ago.

Claims to Fame: the inhabitants of Swiss lake districts reportedly baked with wheat from approximately 6700 BC. Today wheat flour is quite simply the most important ingredient in the bakery. It provides bulk and structure to most of the baker's products, including breads, cakes, biscuits and pastries.

Composition: a grain of wheat consists of three main parts — the endosperm, bran and germ.

■ **Endosperm (85%)** — the white part of the wheat grain from which white flour is milled once the bran and germ have been removed. It consists largely of:

- ■ tightly packed starch granules;
- ■ soluble proteins (albumens);
- ■ insoluble gluten-forming proteins (glutenin and gliadin);
- ■ oil;
- ■ moisture;
- ■ minerals.

Together, glutenin and gliadin bring much-needed elastic, extensible properties to baking. In a bread dough, they act to develop gluten when water has been added and the dough mixed sufficiently. The development of gluten gives strength, structure and volume to a baked product. The suitability of a flour for bakery products is determined by the quality of the gluten and in some cases the quantity it contains.

■ **Bran (13%)** — the outside skin of the wheat grain. Bran consists of six different principal layers, with roles ranging from protection to colouring and enzyme actions. During the milling of white flour the bran layers are largely removed, as bran damages the gluten network that is crucial for bread-making, acting like tiny pieces of glass within an unbaked product. Bran is blended back into finely ground endosperm (white flour) to produce wholemeal flour.

■ **Germ (2%)** — located inside the wheat grain, this is the embryo from which wheat can reproduce itself. It is removed in the milling of white flour as the oil within the germ soon becomes rancid and the enzymes are detrimental to fermentation in bread-making. However, it is blended back into the endosperm and bran to produce wholemeal flour. The germ is rich in oil, calcium, vitamin B and enzymes.

Varieties and Derivatives: wheat flour comes in numerous forms, each designed for a specific reason or kind of baked product.

Flour that contains a good quality and quantity of gluten is known as strong flour. It is beneficial in making bread, yeast-raised baking and puff pastry. Heavy fruitcakes are sometimes made using strong flours. Flour that contains a lower quality and quantity of gluten is known as soft flour.

STRONG FLOUR %	CONSTITUENTS	SOFT FLOUR %
70	Starch	72
13	Insoluble gluten-forming proteins	8
13–15	Moisture	13–15
2.5	Sugar	2.5
1–1.5	Fat	1–1.5
1	Soluble proteins	1
0.5	Mineral salts	0.5

■ **Bread Flour** — a common name for strong flour.

■ **Standard Flour** — milled to provide medium strength for use in baking such items as short pastry products and powder-aerated goods (scones, light fruitcakes, muffins, biscuits and slices).

■ **Self-Raising Flour** — usually a medium-strength flour into which has been blended a proportion of baking powder, at approximately 2% of the flour. It is used for batters, scones, pikelets, cakes and similar baking. Self-raising flour is mainly used when it is difficult to weigh baking powder due to the small amount required. A simple recipe for self-raising flour is:

250g (2 cups) standard plain flour
15g (3 teaspoons) baking powder
Sift these two ingredients together at least seven times.

■ **Wholemeal Flour** — milled from the whole wheat-grain; it contains the bran and germ. It is suitable for all bread and yeast-raised baking, pastries, cakes and biscuits. However, when using wholemeal flour in a recipe, keep in mind that bran damages the gluten network and that this may need to be counteracted.

■ **Semolina Flour** — coarsely ground endosperm that can be used for thickening pie fillings, dusting the baker's peel (shovel) to help transfer breads onto the oven's hearth, and as an ingredient in crusty breads.

■ **Gluten Flour** — dried protein (gluten) from within wheat flour. Given the strength of New Zealand-milled flour, it is needed in doughs made with low-gluten flour (such as rye) or in bread-related recipes that have large quantities of enriching and softening products such as fats, sugar, grains and liquids.

■ **Organic Flour** — milled from organically grown wheat. This wheat is grown by selected farmers and not cross-contaminated with any wheat that has been treated with chemical sprays or other non-organic substances. Commercial flour mills are unable to process organic grains in conjunction with other grains, so organic flour is produced in dedicated organic flour mills. Most baked products can be made using organic flours. Quality is sometimes variable.

Rye Flour

Origin: the cereal rye.

Claims to Fame: the third most popular flour after white and wholemeal wheat flour. Rye breads are by far the most popular breads in Germany and Eastern Europe.

Rye flour contains some flour proteins but these do not form gluten. As a result, breads made with 100% rye flour will be sticky at the dough stage and heavy and dense after baking.

Spelt Flour

Origin: the spelt grain, found by archaeologists in many prehistoric sites. Today it is grown commercially.

Claims to Fame: makes marvellous bread with a rich, nutty flavour. May be tolerated by people with wheat allergies. Although it comes from the same family as wheat, it has a different genetic structure and is higher in protein, vitamins and minerals. Spelt is popular as an organic flour.

Cornflour

Origin: the cereal maize. Not to be confused with wheaten cornflour, which is a wheat extract.

Claims to Fame: used mainly as a thickening agent for custards, sauces and fillings. Almost 100% starch, cornflour does not contain any insoluble gluten-forming proteins. Also known as cornstarch.

Cornmeal

Origin: the kernels of the corn or maize plant. Yellow cornmeal is made from the whole kernels and ground to a fine, medium or coarse texture.

Claims to Fame: best-known in association with polenta (Italy) and cornbread (America). White cornmeal is also available; it has much less beta-carotene than the yellow variety.

Rice Flour

Origin: the cereal rice.

Claims to Fame: assists in absorbing liquids; noted for its keeping qualities and promotion of crispness. Rice flour is added to shortbread and other biscuit and cake recipes. It is almost 100% starch and does not contain any insoluble gluten-forming proteins.

Soy Flour

Origin: the soya bean.

Claims to Fame: very high in fat, making it an excellent ingredient for bread recipes that require keeping qualities, even texture and increased volume. Soy flour is also very rich in protein but does not contain any insoluble gluten-forming proteins.

Malt Products

Origin: barley and (less famously) wheat. Malt is produced in an industrial process called malting, which changes the grain so that it releases enzymes. These include amylases, which convert the starch of the grain into sugars.

Claims to Fame: the major users of malt products worldwide are brewers and the liquor industry: malt is central to the making of both beer and whisky. Non-aficionados of these beverages know malt as a mild natural sweetener, and in baking, malt products are an important food source for yeast. They improve volume, texture, colour, flavour and keeping qualities.

Whole and Kibbled Grains

Origin: various cereals.

Claims to Fame: the ingredients that give 'wholegrain bread' its name. The grains need soaking for at least 12 hours in equal quantities of water to grain to soften them before use.

Composition: whole grains are unmilled; kibbled grains are whole grains that have been cut into smaller pieces.

Salt

Origin: bodies of water such as seas and salt lakes around the world. Salt deposits that now lie underground (rock salt) were formed when seawater evaporated millions of years ago.

Claims to Fame: best known as a flavour enhancer or seasoning. Historically, its value was such that it was used as a currency. Most importantly for bakers, however, it strengthens the gluten structure and makes it more stretchable — and it controls the rate of fermentation within yeast-raised doughs.

Salt is hygroscopic (it absorbs water from the air). It should be stored away from moisture and — even more importantly — should never be placed in direct contact with yeast, as it will take moisture from yeast cells and ultimately kill them.

Composition: the chemical elements sodium and chloride.

Varieties: table salt, sea salt, iodised salt, vacuum salt and rock salt (the latter mainly used for decoration due to its large crystal size).

Eggs

Origin: *Gallus domesticus* (chickens). Also ducks, guinea fowl and other poultry.

Claims to Fame: the 'incredible edible egg' of many international marketing campaigns is undergoing a renaissance or a rehabilitation. In baking, however, the egg never went away.

Eggs are high in nutrients and — for the baker — cost: they are used in large quantities in bakeries and are more expensive than many other ingredients.

Any baker needs a good understanding of eggs, which have moisturising, aeration, structural, emulsifying, keeping and glazing properties as well as nutritional qualities and a distinctive flavour. The size of eggs can affect a recipe, so it is often necessary to weigh them (after discarding the shells).

Composition: a whole egg consists of a yolk, a white and a shell. Egg whites are known as albumen. Eggs are 73% water. Their significant nutrients include protein (both yolks and whites) and fat (yolks only).

Varieties and Derivatives: commercial bakeries use various processed forms of egg as well as the traditional shell egg. The shell egg is the only form used in this book.

Milk

Origin: bovine quadrupeds of the *Bos* genus (cattle).

Claims to Fame: even more of a staple in the Western diet than eggs. For the baker it offers moisture, texture, colour, eating qualities and keeping qualities as well as its proven nutritional properties.

Fresh milk should always be kept in the refrigerator and the use-by date adhered to.

Composition: whole milk (also known as full-cream milk) is fresh milk as it comes from the cow, with nothing added or removed. It contains 3.5% fat (known as milk fat), 8.5% non-fat milk solids and 88% water. It is high in protein and several other nutrients, notably calcium.

Varieties and Derivatives: many, including milk powders, condensed milk and evaporated milk.

■ **Fresh Cream** — obtained from the fat content of the cow's milk. Fresh cream is seldom used as a liquid in doughs or batters, except in a few specialty products. It is more important in the production of fillings, toppings, dessert sauces and cold desserts such as mousses.

When whipped, cream should double its original volume.

■ **Butter** — by far the best-known fat. If butter is used in baking, a top-quality product is virtually guaranteed. Some recipes call for hard, softened or even melted butter; use of the wrong one can affect the quality of baking.

Baking Powder

Origin and Composition: cream of tartar and bicarbonate of soda — an acid and an alkali.

Claims to Fame: 'sure to rise', according to a Lyttelton grocer (who gave his name to a New Zealand brand that has since become iconic). Baking powder is responsible for the aeration, the final volume and often the crumb structure of cakes and other baking, including quick breads — so-called because their baking powder content enables the baker to dispense with both yeast and kneading.

Baking powder becomes moist during mixing and heating in the oven. This prompts the acid and alkali to react, producing carbon dioxide. The gas lifts and pushes up the final dough or batter until the proteins from the eggs and flour have coagulated (set) during baking.

All batters and doughs containing baking powder should be kept cool (21°C or below) to prevent the gas from doing its work too early. Ideally, they should be baked immediately after being mixed.

Sugar

Origin: cane and beet sugar provide most of what we know as sugar (sucrose). Both are natural, plant-derived substances.

Composition: sugar belongs to the group of organic compounds called carbohydrates.

Claims to Fame: the world's best-known sweetener. Actually it's a spice — though it's used much less sparingly than most. Crusaders brought sugar to Europe in the eleventh century but it remained a rare luxury there until the fifteenth century.

Most of today's sugar crops are used by the international food industry, although non-food-related industries such as tanning and plastics manufacturing use a small amount of sugar.

As well as sweetening baked products, sugar creates tenderness by weakening the gluten structure, provides food for yeast during fermentation, caramelises and gives crust colour, and acts as a creaming agent with fats and a foaming agent with eggs. Like salt, sugar is hygroscopic and should be stored away from moisture.

Varieties: sugar is refined into grains and syrups. The grains include caster sugar, granulated sugar (ordinary white sugar), brown sugar, raw sugar, icing sugar (granulated sugar crushed to powder with starch added). Among the syrups are golden syrup, molasses and treacle.

Spices

Origin: various parts of different plants.

Claims to Fame: the earliest known mention of spices is in an Assyrian myth, which claims the gods drank sesame-spiced wine the night before they made the earth. The brothers of Joseph sold him to spice merchants, Hippocrates listed spices as active ingredients in medicines, a major spice-trade route traversed the deserts of southern Asia and the Middle East, and wars broke out over control of the spice trade.

Known to cooks as aromatic or pungent plant matter used to flavour food, spices are a great example of the idea that good things come in small packages. Flavourwise, they pack a punch, so bakers should use them sparingly.

Spices are generally available whole or ground. The latter lose their flavour rapidly, so it is important to replace them after six months.

Varieties: those used in baking include: from barks — cinnamon, cassia; from buds — cloves; from flowers — rose flower, orange flower; from fruits — chillies, peppers; from roots — ginger; from seeds — nutmeg, sesame, poppy, caraway, aniseed.

Cocoa

Origin: it is more or less true that chocolate grows on trees: cacao trees, *Theobroma cacao*. The trees grow large pods, whose seeds (beans) are fermented, dried, roasted and then processed into cocoa liquor. From this, cocoa powder, cocoa butter and chocolate are made. So it is true to say that cocoa is a spice although, like sugar, it has lost that association — and, to become edible, it undergoes much more processing than most other spices.

Composition: cocoa beans are 54% cocoa butter, 11.5% protein, 9% starch, 5% water. Other ingredients include theobromine and caffeine (both stimulants), and aromatic oils.

Claims to Fame: In Mexico's Aztec empire, cocoa pods were used not only for beverages and as currency but also in human sacrifice. More recent users of cocoa-derived products include another killer, the tobacco industry, but otherwise its applications are restricted to food, drink, cosmetics and natural remedies.

Varieties and Derivatives:

■ **Cocoa Powder** — processed from cocoa liquor, which comes from cocoa beans that are fermented, dried and then roasted. Cocoa contains moisture-absorbing starch, so when it is added to a batter, a reduction of flour is necessary to keep the recipe balanced.

■ **Chocolate Couverture** — much higher in cocoa solids than other chocolate. It is prepared from cocoa butter, cocoa and sugar that have been milled together, and is used in producing top-quality chocolate products. Bakers temper chocolate couverture before working with it; this ensures that the couverture sets with an attractive sheen.

Tempering Chocolate Couverture: Half-fill a saucepan with cold water and bring it to the boil. Meanwhile, break the chocolate into small pieces.

Remove the saucepan from the heat. Place the chocolate in a stainless-steel bowl over the hot water (the bowl must fit inside the saucepan). Do not allow any water or steam to come into contact with the couverture, as this will thicken it and make it unusable.

Stir the chocolate with a clean wooden spoon as it melts, until it has reached 40ºC. (You may need to remove the bowl from the water from time to time to avoid overheating.)

Tip two-thirds of the couverture onto a marble slab or cold bench. Using two palette knives, rotate the chocolate until it has cooled to 27ºC. Place it with the remaining third and mix thoroughly until well combined.

Place the bowl back over the warm water and warm the couverture to exactly 30ºC. Use immediately.

■ **Compound Chocolate (also called chocolate coating)** — prepared from vegetable fats, cocoa powder, sugar, milk solids and emulsifiers. This is much easier to use than couverture and does not require any special treatment beforehand. Dark, milk and white compound chocolate are available.

The quality of Compound Chocolate is not as high as that of Chocolate Couverture.

Melting Compound Chocolate: Half-fill a saucepan with cold water and bring it to the boil. Meanwhile, break the chocolate into small pieces.

Remove the saucepan from the heat. Place the chocolate in a stainless-steel bowl over the hot water (the bowl must fit inside the saucepan). Do not allow any water or steam to come into contact with the compound chocolate, as this will thicken it and make it unusable.

Stir the chocolate with a clean wooden spoon as it melts, until it has reached 40°C. (You may need to remove the bowl from the water from time to time to avoid overheating.)

Use compound chocolate at 40°C; the chocolate will set with an attractive sheen.

Nuts

Origin: plants (mostly trees) cultivated in crops around the world.

Claims to Fame: used extensively in various forms, including oils, for culinary purposes. Nuts also feature in some inedible products: peanuts are used in the making of the explosive nitroglycerin.

Composition: high in fat, which means they have a limited shelf life and will quickly turn rancid if stored incorrectly. They should be kept in a cool place — the freezer, if purchased in large quantities.

Varieties: the following are the most commonly used in baking.

■ **Almonds** — available as whole natural, blanched, split, flaked, nibbed and ground almonds.

■ **Walnuts** — used either chopped or whole for decoration.

■ **Pecans** — are expensive; should be used in top-quality baking.

■ **Peanuts** — a legume, and the only nut to be grown in the ground (hence the alternative name groundnut).

■ **Coconut** — can be used in cakes or biscuits and is often used as a coating or decoration.

■ **Hazelnuts** — have a distinctive flavour and are best if roasted first.

Fruits

Origin: trees, vines, plants and bushes. Botanically, a fruit is an edible, fleshy, seed-bearing structure grown by a perennial — but bakers and botanists see things differently: the baker embraces as fruit some things (such as rhubarb stems) that the botanist would emphatically categorise elsewhere.

Claims to Fame: since its far from promising start in the Garden of Eden, fruit has come a long way, with current 'five-plus a day' campaigns exhorting the citizenry to eat five or more servings of fruit and veges daily. In baking, fruit is used in abundance. Whoever heard of a fruit-free fruitcake?

Varieties: dried fruit and related products commonly used in baking include currants, sultanas, raisins and mixed peel. Figs and dates are among other dried fruits that feature in baked goods. Dried fruit may be prepared for baking by washing, drying, cleaning (removing stones and stalks), and soaking in water or alcohol.

Fresh, tinned and frozen fruit used in baking include apples, pears, apricots, grapes, cherries and berries such as strawberries, raspberries, blackcurrants and blueberries.

Formulas and Measurements

Bakers generally talk about formulas rather than recipes. If this sounds more like chemistry than cookery, it is because a bakery is very much like a chemistry laboratory — both in the scientific accuracy of the procedures and in the complex reactions that take place during the mixing and baking. In France, pâtisseries are often called laboratories.

Weight and Volume

■ All ingredients must be measured accurately. In bread-making, most ingredients are weighed. (See 'Measuring' in the Breads chapter, page 43, for more information about this.)

Water, liquid milk and beaten eggs may be measured by volume — although if quantities are large, it is advisable to weigh them on an accurate set of scales. With these ingredients, 1kg is the same as 1 litre. Not all liquids have this weight–volume equivalency, so do not assume that you can always substitute measurements by volume for measurements by weight (or vice versa).

All teaspoon measurements in this book are based on level teaspoons.

Recipe Balance

■ As recipes are balanced formulations, adding too much of one ingredient will upset the balance of the recipe, affecting other ingredients.

Special care must be taken when weighing salt, baking powder, spices, sugar and other ingredients used in small quantities. Where recipes specify a small quantity, this often means that a little of the ingredient goes a long way, and that its effect on the finished baked product is significant.

Baker's Percentages

■ Commercial bakers use a simple but versatile system of percentages for expressing their formulas or recipes. Baker's percentages indicate the quantities that would be required of each ingredient if 100kg of flour comprised 100%. Thus, each ingredient is expressed as a percentage of the total flour weight or, in other words, the percentage of each ingredient is its total weight divided by the weight of the flour, multiplied by 100. For example:

$$\frac{\text{Total weight of ingredient}}{\text{Total weight of flour}} \times 100 = \% \text{ of ingredient}$$

The flour is always expressed as 100%. If two kinds of flour are used, their total is still 100%. Any ingredient that weighs the same as the flour is also expressed as 100%.

To help understand how baker's percentages are used, see the following recipes and check their figures with the equation above.

Basic White Bread Recipe

INGREDIENT	WEIGHT	%
Bread flour	5.000 kg	100
Salt	0.100 kg	2
Sugar	0.050 kg	1
Fat	0.150 kg	3
Yeast	0.150 kg	3
Water	2.800 lt	56
Total weight	8.250 kg	
Yield @ 0.550 kg	15	

Basic Cake Recipe

INGREDIENT	WEIGHT	%
Cake flour	2.500 kg	100
Sugar	2.500 kg	100
Baking powder	0.125 kg	5
Salt	0.063 kg	2.5
Shortening	1.250 kg	50
Milk	1.500 lt	60
Egg whites	1.500 lt	60
Total weight	9.438 kg	
Yield @ 0.500 kg	18.8	

The advantages of using baker's percentages are that the formulations or recipes are easy to adapt for any yield, and single ingredients may be varied or other ingredients added without changing the whole formulation. For example, if you add blueberries to a muffin formulation, the percentages of all the other ingredients can stay the same.

The recipes in this book have been written so you can follow them without worrying about baker's percentages. However, advanced bakers may find these charts helpful.

Metric Conversions
All recipes in this book use the metric system of measurements.

To convert ounces (oz) to grams (g)
Conversion: 1oz = 28.4g
Example: 16oz x 28.4g = 454.4g

To convert pounds (lb) to kilograms (kg)
Conversion: 1lb = 0.454g (1lb = 16oz)
Example: 1lb 3oz = 19oz x 28.4g = 0.539kg

To convert Celsius (°C) to Fahrenheit (°F)
Formula: F − 32 ÷ 9 x 5 = C
Example: 425°F (− 32 ÷ 9 x 5) = 218°C

To convert Fahrenheit (°F) to Celsius (°C)
Formula: C ÷ 5 x 9 + 32 = F
Example: 218°C (÷ 5 x 9 + 32) = 424°F

Oven Temperature Equivalents

GAS MARK	FAHRENHEIT	CELSIUS	DESCRIPTION
	212	100	Very Cool
½	265	130	Very Cool
1	290	145	Very Cool
2	310	155	Cool
3	335	170	Warm
4	355	180	Moderate or Medium
5	380	195	Moderately Hot or Medium-Hot
6	400	205	Moderately Hot or Medium-Hot
7	425	220	Hot
8	445	230	Hot
9	470	245	Very Hot
10	482	250	Very Hot

These temperatures relate to the approximate heat at the centre of the oven. The Celsius temperatures have been rounded up or down to the nearest 5°C.

Glossary

Some of the terms explained in this glossary do not appear elsewhere in this book. However, they are included here to help bakers understand the terminology commonly used in baking.

Aeration — incorporation of air or carbon dioxide in a mixture during one or more stages of its preparation. Aeration lightens the mixture and the resulting baked item. Air can be introduced by whisking, beating or mixing. Carbon dioxide can be introduced by baking powder or yeast.

Albumen — the protein of eggs found in the egg white.

Almond Paste — a mixture of ground almonds, sugar and sufficient egg to form a firm, pliable paste that is used to ice cakes or in pastries and sweets. Similar to marzipan but less sweet and pliable.

Baking Blind — baking an unfilled flan or tart pastry cases. This is done by lining the pastry base with baking paper fitting snugly into the corners, filling it with rice or dried beans and baking until the pastry has set or turned golden-brown in colour. The paper and beans are removed and a filling is added.

Baking Powder — chemicals that, when moistened and heated, generate carbon dioxide, aerating cakes and biscuits. See also the Ingredients chapter.

Baking Temperature — refers to the correct control of temperatures in baking. Usually expressed in either Gas Mark, degrees Celsius (°C) or degrees Fahrenheit (°F).

Baking Time — how long an item should be baked in an oven at correctly controlled temperatures. Usually expressed in minutes and/or hours.

Batter — usually a soft cake mixture. A basic cake batter can consist of butter, sugar, eggs, milk and flour.

Beating — often done with a mixture of ingredients to aerate them. Can be achieved using a simple wooden spoon or an electric mixer.

Bloom — indicates a healthy shine or sparkle on baked goods. With chocolate, a fat or sugar bloom is a whitish coating that can result from under- or over-heating during the melting stage.

Bran — hard outer covering of wheat and other grains. Once milled, it can be used in baking.

Bread Flour — flour milled from hard wheat. It has a high protein content and is generally used for producing yeast-raised goods. Also called strong flour.

Brioche — French term for a yeast dough that is rich, containing large quantities of eggs and butter. This is also the name of the finished products.

Bulk Fermentation — the period of time during which a yeasted dough is allowed to ferment in bulk. Also called first rising.

Bun Wash — liquid brushed on yeast buns, immediately after removal from the oven, to achieve a glaze or shine. Usually made up of sugar and water that have been boiled together.

Butter Cream — icing made of butter blended with icing sugar or a simple sugar syrup. Flavours and colours are sometimes added.

Cake — baked mixture of butter or margarine, sugar, eggs, liquids, flour, etc.

Cake Flour — milled from soft wheat, which has a low to medium protein content and is generally used for cakes and sometimes biscuits and cookies. Also called soft flour.

Caramel — sugar that is boiled to reach a temperature above 155°C. The process turns it amber-brown in colour.

Caramelisation — the browning effect of heat on sugars.

Carbon Dioxide (CO₂) — Baking powder and yeast fermentation produce this gas, thus aerating baked goods such as cakes, breads and biscuits.

Caster Sugar — sugar that has been finely ground so that it will dissolve quickly and easily when baked goods are prepared. The granule size is between that of icing sugar and granulated sugar.

Celsius — metric scale by which temperature is measured, with 0°C the freezing point and 100°C the boiling point for water at sea level.

Coagulation — setting of a protein, usually by heat; for example, the setting of the protein (gluten) in flour during baking.

Cocoa — dry powder that remains after cocoa butter is pressed out of chocolate liquor.

Cocoa, Dutch Process — see Dutch Process Cocoa.

Cocoa Butter — white or yellowish fat found in natural chocolate.

Compound Chocolate — chocolate coating made from vegetable fats rather than cocoa butter, used for dipping, moulding and coating of bakery goods.

Confectioner's Sugar — see Icing Sugar.

Couverture — natural, sweet chocolate containing no fats other than natural cocoa butter, used for dipping, moulding and coating of bakery goods.

Creaming — the process of beating fats and sugar together to blend them uniformly and to incorporate air. Used in the making of cakes, cookies and biscuits.

Crème Pâtissière — thick custard containing eggs, milk, sugar, vanilla and flour.

Curdling — undesirable separation of ingredients such as fat, sugar and eggs that have been combined by beating or stirring. Usually caused by adding the liquid too quickly or when it's too cold. Sometimes called splitting.

Decorating — adding fruits, nuts, chocolate and/or icing to embellish a baked product.

Depositing — placing portions of cake batter into cake tins by hand or machine. The latter is called a depositer.

Developing — mixing a dough thoroughly to increase the elasticity and extensibility of the gluten (protein in flour).

Dividing — separating dough or cake batters into the desired sizes and weights before baking, using scales as necessary. Also called Scaling.

Docking — piercing or pricking pastry or dough before baking. This allows steam to escape, so prevents blistering in pastries, and adds a decorative effect on breads.

Dough — usually refers to a mixture of flour and water, which may or may not be combined with yeast.

Dusting — sprinkling flour or icing sugar onto a work surface to prevent a dough or paste from sticking, or using a fine-mesh sieve to sprinkle icing sugar over the top of a baked product for decoration.

Dutch Process Cocoa — cocoa that has been processed with an alkali to reduce its acidity, creating a milder flavour.

Egg Wash — beaten eggs, usually diluted with water or milk. Brushed on, before or after baking, to achieve a glazed surface.

Emulsifier — an ingredient that assists in combining two substances or ingredients that don't normally mix together (as below). Emulsifiers also help increase the shelf life of baked goods.

Emulsion — a uniform mixture of two substances or ingredients that don't normally mix together. An example is the fats and eggs within a cake batter: the lecithin in the egg is an effective natural emulsifier.

Endosperm — the white part of the wheat grain. White flour is milled from the endosperm once the bran and germ have been removed. See also the Ingredients chapter.

Enrobing — coating a cake or other baked item with icing or chocolate.

Essences — compounds used for flavouring bakery products. Can be either natural, artificial or blends of both.

Fahrenheit — non-metric scale for measuring temperature, with 32°F the freezing point of water and 212°F its boiling point.

Ferment — mixture of water, yeast and flour allowed to ferment at controlled temperatures and times, for use in yeasted dough. Also called Sponge.

Fermentation — process by which yeast changes carbohydrates into carbon dioxide and alcohol. The gas aerates fermented yeast products; the alcohol plays a role in flavour. See also 'How It Works' in the Breads chapter.

Firm Dough — contains comparatively little liquid, making it firm. Also called a tight dough.

First Rising — see Bulk Fermentation.

Flan — an open pastry case filled with a savoury or sweet filling and baked in a hoop or tin.

Fondant — icing made with boiled sugar, water and glucose, mixed so that it sets in a mass of extremely small white crystals.

Frangipane — an almond-flavoured cream made with butter, sugar, eggs and ground almonds and used as a filling in desserts and pastries. Often contains additional almond flavouring.

Ganache — rich chocolate cream made with boiled cream and high-quality chocolate. It can be melted, cooled and then used as a glaze, or whipped and used as a filling.

Gelatinisation — the heating of starch with water, resulting in a thick, jelly-like paste when the mixture cools.

Genoise — a sponge cake made with eggs, sugar, flour and melted butter. A base for gâteaux.

Germ — located inside the wheat grain; the embryo from which wheat can reproduce itself.

Glaze — a shiny coating, such as a syrup, jam or egg wash applied to bakery products before or after baking.

Gliadin — an elastic protein found in wheat. It combines with another protein, glutenin, to form gluten.

Gluten — an elastic, insoluble substance formed by two proteins (gliadin and glutenin) that are present in wheat. When mixed with liquid, it gives structure and strength to baked products.

Glutenin — an extensible protein found in wheat that combines with another protein, gliadin, to form gluten.

Glycerine — colourless and odourless syrup with a sweet taste, used in cakes to prevent them from becoming stale.

Icing Sugar —sugar that has been ground to a powder and generally mixed with a little cornflour or starch to prevent caking (sticking). Also called confectioner's sugar or powdered sugar.

Intermediate Proof — a resting period of 10–15 minutes that takes place between the rounding and final make-up or shaping of a yeasted bread dough, allowing the gluten network to relax. Sometimes referred to as first proof, recovery time or resting time.

Knock Back — during bulk fermentation of a yeasted dough, the baker gently knocks it back to prevent the premature escape of carbon dioxide. This is done by hand and involves pushing, and folding the dough very gently, generally three-quarters of the way through the bulk fermentation period.

Lamination — the layering of fat and dough, as used in making puff pastry, croissants or Danish pastries.

Lean Dough — yeasted dough that is low in fat and sugar.

Lecithin — a powerful emulsifying agent, naturally found in egg yolks.

Levain Starter — made by combining wild yeast spores (captured from the air) with flour and water. The mixture is allowed to ferment over a long period and is then mixed with more flour and other ingredients to make a sourdough or 'pain au levain' dough. Also called a sourdough starter.

Macaroon — a cookie made of egg whites and almond paste or coconut.

Macerating — soaking in liquid in order to soften. Generally applied to dried fruits that are sprinkled with liqueur or other alcohol to improve their flavour.

Malt Flour — flour made from sprouted wheat or barley. Malt products can be an important food source for yeast in yeast-raised doughs.

Malt Syrup — type of syrup containing maltose sugar, extracted from sprouted wheat or barley.

Marzipan — ground almonds and sugar, mixed together with sufficient egg to form a firm, pliable paste. Similar to almond paste but sweeter and more pliable, it is often shaped into decorations (such as small animals) and applied to icing on cakes.

Masking — covering the sides and/or surface of a cake or gâteau with icing, toasted nuts, chocolate shavings, etc.

Molasses — heavy brown syrup made from cane sugar.

Mould — hollow form made from metal, plaster, plastic or wood in which a dough, jelly or other food can be shaped. Also, fungi that grow in favourable conditions (warmth and moisture), frequently on food.

Moulding — shaping a piece of dough or paste.

Mousse — a soft, creamy dessert that is made light by the addition of whipped cream and/or egg whites.

No-Time Dough — bread dough made with a large quantity of yeast and a short fermentation time, usually in conjunction with a specific improving agent.

Old Dough — dough that has been over-fermented. It can be used in a fresh dough to increase the flavour.

Oven Spring — the rise of a yeasted dough in the oven due to the heat-prompted expansion of the gases inside the dough.

Pain au Levain — classic French bread made with natural yeast starter (levain), salt, flour and water. See also Levain Starter.

Palette Knife — a special knife that has a thin, flat blade with a rounded end. Used for spreading icings, jams, creams and similar substances.

Pasteurisation — heating process used to kill bacteria that might cause disease or spoilage in food.

Pastry Cream — see Crème Pâtissière.

Peel — flat wooden shovel used to place oven-bottom (hearth) breads and baked products in an oven and to remove them. Also, candied rinds of citrus fruits (lemon or orange peel).

Petit Four — a delicate cake, biscuit or pastry small enough to be eaten in one or two bites. A petit four sec is dry (as in biscuit) and a petit four glacé is finished with icing.

Pie — a foodstuff usually baked in a dish or tin. May feature a pastry base and top with a filling containing fruit, meat, vegetables, fish, etc.

Piping — forcing a soft mixture, usually a batter or icing, through a piping bag fitted with a piping tube. Used to fill or make decorative patterns on bakery products.

Piping Bag — cone-shaped bag made of plastic or nylon with a piping tube to force soft mixtures out for filling or decorating purposes. Also called a pastry or savoy bag.

Piping Tube — nozzle made of metal or plastic and fitted in the end of a piping bag. Piping tubes come in various sizes and can be plain or shaped.

Prove — term used to explain the action of yeast. Yeast produces carbon dioxide, thereby causing breads, buns or rolls to rise before they are baked.

Prover — cabinet in which yeasted goods are placed to prove before baking. The cabinet must be warm and humid for this to happen.

Puff Pastry — layers of fat and dough that have been created by folding and turning the pastry on itself several times. Also called flaky pastry.

Recipe — formula containing quantities of ingredients used for a particular product and information including make-up procedures, yields, temperatures, times and special techniques.

Resting Time — required for doughs and pastries to relax after intensive mixing or handling. This is an important stage as it often allows the next part of production to flow smoothly, causing no stress to the mixture.

Retarding — refrigeration of a yeasted dough to slow the fermentation down, enhancing the flavour, structure and eating qualities.

Rounding — a method of moulding a piece of dough into a round ball with a smooth skin or surface.

Scaling — see Dividing.

Self-Raising Flour — a mixture of flour and baking powder, sifted together at least seven times. Also called scone flour or, in the United States, self-rising flour. The proportions are: 250g (2 cups) standard flour and 15g (3 teaspoons) baking powder.

Short Pastry — a firm mixture made from flour, fat or butter, eggs or liquids. May also contain sugar, salt and baking powder. It can be either sweet (called sweet pastry) or savoury.

Skinning — the undesirable formation of a dry skin on unbaked dough, caused by a dry atmosphere; it prevents a glossy crust from forming when the dough is baked. Skinning can be prevented by covering the dough during bulk fermentation and other pre-baking stages.

Slack Dough — dough containing sufficient liquids to make it soft to the touch (by comparison with a Firm Dough).

Soft Flour — milled from soft wheat with low gluten content. Generally used for cakes and biscuits. See also Cake Flour.

Sourdough — yeasted dough made with a starter that has fermented long enough to become sour and acidic in flavour. It is also a name for the baked loaf, for example San Francisco Sourdough.

Sponge — see Ferment.

Sponge Cake — type of cake made by whisking eggs and sugar to a foam and then folding in flour.

Strong Flour — flour milled from hard wheat. It has a high protein content and is generally used for yeast-raised baking. Also called Bread Flour.

Tart — see Flan.

Turntable — rotating base on which a cake or other foodstuff is placed for the application of icing or cream (or to be served to various guests seated around a table). Also called a Lazy Susan.

Yield — number of units or portions expected from a recipe, based on a predetermined size or weight.

Zest — outside rind of a citrus fruit. Contains essential oils of the fruit.

Index